RAISING GLOBAL IQ

RAISING GLOBAL IQ

Preparing Our Students for a Shrinking Planet

Carl F. Hobert

Beacon Press
Boston

Beacon Press
25 Beacon Street
Boston, Massachusetts 02108-2892
www.beacon.org

Beacon Press books
are published under the auspices of
the Unitarian Universalist Association of Congregations.

Printed in the United States of America

16 15 14 13 8 7 6 5 4 3 2 1

This book is printed on acid-free paper that meets the uncoated paper
ANSI/NISO specifications for permanence as revised in 1992.

Text design and composition by Kim Arney

Library of Congress Cataloging-in-Publication Data

Hobert, Carl F.
Raising global IQ : preparing our students for a shrinking planet / Carl Hobert.
p. cm.
Includes bibliographical references and index.
ISBN 978-0-8070-3288-6 (hardback)
1. International education. 2. Education and globalization. 3. Moral education.
I. Title.
LC1090.H63 2013
370.116—dc23 2012029801

To my three magical daughters, Leah, Olivia, and Juliana, for offering me their deep love and for teaching me the best lessons of compassion I have ever learned. And to my dear mother and late father, whose unconditional love and belief in opening their three sons' eyes to a shrinking world deeply influenced me from an early age.

—CFH

To Friendship among Children and Youth around the World (founded under UNESCO), New York:

You young people should consider yourselves fortunate that you, in your impressionable years, have the opportunity to exchange viewpoints and ideas with those of a variety of cultural backgrounds. There is no better opportunity to acquire the life-long insights that are necessary for the resolution of international problems and conflicts.

In the hope that your endeavors have a lasting impact, I send you my warmest greetings and wishes.

—Albert Einstein,
Salzburg, Austria,
November 22, 1952

Contents

Foreword

Over a century ago, H. G. Wells wrote that "history is a race between education and catastrophe." In many ways, education is winning that race. More people are literate, healthy, and well-nourished today than ever before in human history. Fewer people have died in wars over the past generation than during most comparable periods. The hands of the clock of nuclear holocaust have been turned back.

At the same time, the race has become swifter. Technology has knit the world more closely together. Global companies design, produce, and market goods and services with little consideration of national boundaries. Millions of people from one part of the world are migrating to another part. Once-underdeveloped countries such as China, India, Brazil, Indonesia, and Turkey are now important powers. Their young people are far better educated than ever before. Events in one part of the world that would once have had only regional impact now influence the lives of everyone on the planet.

Take the current crisis in the Eurozone. Financial, economic, and structural problems in the small nation of Greece, and to a lesser extent in countries such as Ireland, Portugal, Spain, and Italy, could potentially derail the entire world economy. Whether or not today's US high school and university graduates face bleak or upbeat employment prospects over the next several years could depend on decisions made in Berlin and Brussels, regardless of how well or how poorly policy is managed in Washington and New York.

For the past fifty years, thoughtful people have realized that more and more elements of our lives are becoming more and more globally influenced. Take climate change, the management of epidemic diseases, or the price of food. The forests of the American West are unprecedentedly fragile: tinder-dry, infested by invasive new species, and threatening to destroy entire communities. The H1N1 virus has faded from the headlines, but public-health leaders throughout the world continue to have nightmares that viruses infecting a flock of chickens or geese in China or Indonesia will mutate into an uncontainable human epidemic. The price of fish goes up and up as we fail to establish a meaningful and enforceable law of the seas to ensure sustainability. The list could go on and on, but the basic point is that the impact of global forces on our lives is so pervasive that almost every American is now aware that the world of our parents and grandparents has changed irrevocably.

This is understandably disturbing to almost everyone. It is very challenging to manage these complex issues on a global basis. Most fundamentally, the system of global decision making continues to be dominated by sovereign nation-states with the mandate to look after their own interests. This is why, for example, it has been so difficult to find a solution to the Euro crisis. The ongoing gap between global forces and national power structures and identities demands that the next generation have the knowledge, attitudes, and skills to understand and influence multinational issues and groups in an informed and competent way.

Raising Global IQ: Preparing Our Students for a Shrinking Planet lays out a detailed and practical blueprint for how we can prepare our next generation of citizens with the tools they will need to sustain the optimism, freedom, leadership, and opportunity that have marked American life from its founding. We undertake this challenging task from a position of many strengths. First, we are a society that has always looked to a better future with a willingness to change yesterday's patterns in order to achieve it. Second, we are the world's most diverse and multicultural society, and virtually every neighborhood, town, and school in America provides, even demands, engagement with other languages and cultures. Third, the opportunity to travel and visit other countries has never before been more affordable or widely available. Once the purview of a wealthy elite, travel to other countries is now offered through many school programs, church groups, and even sports teams, often with scholarship or fund-raising or work options available. Social networking and technology are opening up whole new worlds of opportunity to engage with people from other countries. The overseas "pen pal" of yesteryear is being replaced by Facebook, Twitter, and cell-phone connections that can bring instantaneous audio and visual engagement with hundreds if not thousands of people around the world. And, as Carl Hobert points out, within the past decade or two we have already demonstrated how schools, communities, and households can incorporate transformational change in the way we have positively incorporated new technologies and increased diversity in our school curricula and our lives.

So we enter this period of great change with much strength, and the well-being of the next generation depends on how successfully we provide it with the knowledge and experience necessary for leadership in a global age. As Hobert points out, this can no longer be left for a select few to experience at the college and university level. The very best time to begin learning a second language, and indeed to begin engaging with people from other cultures, is at the preschool, kindergarten, and elementary levels.

Raising Global IQ provides a detailed and user-friendly compendium of both the general categories and specific activities that would enable a school administrator, a teacher, a parent, or a student to understand what the "end-game" of global competence looks like and what broadly needs to be done to get there, and it gives concrete examples of how others have improved the global IQ of their own communities.

Specifically, Hobert sees five areas where our schools will need to do things differently going forward if we expect to sustain our global leadership throughout the twenty-first century: 1) language and cultural fluency, including Chinese, Arabic, and other non-western languages, as well as the more traditional European languages; 2) technology and media as a means to making international issues more alive in the classroom; 3) expanded international exchange programs and other forms of cross-cultural engagement; 4) problem solving and participatory case studies of global crises, such as the one currently taking place in Syria; 5) and service-learning opportunities, both here at home and through well-thought-out programs abroad.

Strengthening these curriculum and content areas would not only improve a school's global IQ but would also enhance the school's general problem-solving skills and the capacity to apply classroom learning to life experience.

Most schools are already doing most of these activities to a greater or lesser extent; they are not the monopoly of wealthy or advanced schools, communities, or families. Raising the global IQ of a school system need not cost a lot more money than is currently being spent or require radical reform of the curriculum or extracurricular activities. However, the global demands of the next twenty-five years will require that we better integrate and more systematically and consistently deliver the international components of our K–12 education. Hobert makes an important point when he suggests that school systems would benefit greatly from establishing the position of Director of Global Programs or International Studies to bring coherence and accountability to the raising of global IQ, just as we have so often done with educational technology.

I would argue that the greatest challenge of the next generation will be managing global opportunities and challenges from a nationally based system of decision making. This will require young people with the global IQ necessary to produce positive results while working with individuals of different languages and cultures. America is well positioned to be able to do this, and the well-being of our country depends upon it. Carl Hobert, with *Raising Global IQ*, has provided us with an invaluable roadmap on how to prepare our children for the new world they will inevitably inhabit.

—Charles MacCormack

Dr. Charles F. MacCormack is former president and chief executive officer of Save the Children Federation, Inc. He now serves as board chair of InterAction and as a director of Malaria No More.

Introduction

Improving Our Schools' Global Intelligence Quotient

It was a crisp and sunny New England autumn morning in 2002, and I had arrived early at the school where I taught. I wanted to correct students' French and Spanish quizzes and tests, long overdue; catch up on e-mails; write classroom assignments on the whiteboard for my beginning, intermediate, and advanced modern language classes; and still have time to meet some colleagues over coffee before our teaching day began. By 7:30 a.m., I headed out of my classroom to join other teachers and administrators in the small but bright faculty dining room.

En route, I leaned down to pick up the newspapers that had been delivered outside our school library earlier that morning, wrapped in blue plastic bags, and covered with a bit of dew. As I walked down the brick hallway in front of the still-locked library entrance, slowly pulling the newspapers from their bags, I said, "*Bonjour*!" "*Buenos días*!" and "*Ni hao*!" to several of the middle and upper school students sitting comfortably on three wooden benches on one side of the hallway. "How was your scrimmage yesterday?" I asked two of the boys who had moved on to the varsity ranks that fall from the freshman football team that I co-coached. "How did you like that weekend drama program?" I asked two other boys who were seated there, both extremely talented actors. "It was amazing," one of them said. "We're destined to act on Broadway one day!" As he smiled, the other rolled his eyes and raised his fingers in the "OK" sign, as if to say, "Yeah, right!" Ah, how I loved working with those confident and humble adolescents.

The morning had started so well, I thought, chuckling as I continued on my way to the library door. As I placed the newspapers down in front of the locked door, sliding the slightly wet plastic wrappers off, I glanced at the *New York Times* front page. The headline read: "Suicide Bomber on Jerusalem Bus Kills 11." I started to read the article, stunned, shocked, breathless. My thoughts jolted from practical preoccupations to the details of the bombing. As I read the front-page article, I imagined the children who had died on that Jerusalem bus on their way to school, their cell phones ringing after the blast like a slightly off-key middle school orchestra. Worried mothers and fathers tried to contact their sons and daughters, only to discover later that day that they would never speak to them again. I imagined the ambulances that arrived at the site of that charred, mangled bus—"ORs on wheels" my Israeli friends call them—as trauma specialists and their surgical teams came out of nowhere, in triage-mode, in an attempt to save as many lives as they could. How, I asked myself at that moment, could this happen to children, children like my own three daughters, like the students I had just spoken to in the hall? I felt a tinge of nausea as I contemplated that suicide bombing, depicted so graphically in the *Times* and now frozen in my mind. I placed the newspapers down in front of the library door, but instead of going to get coffee and have my raisin bran, I took a roundabout walk outside to return to my classroom, noticing the ice particles of my quickened breath. I reflected on the news and the increasingly familiar feeling I had of deep sadness and frustrated helplessness in the face of terrible events unfolding in the Middle East and other hot spots around the world. I decided that my soon-to-arrive students and I could at least talk about what had happened so that we could begin to acknowledge the significance of the event even from a distance.

Fifteen minutes later I was broaching the topic with a small group of sixteen- and seventeen-year-old boys, my junior class advisees, for our short, fifteen-minute homeroom period. There was some interest in the topic, yet I found myself surprised that most of the boys seemed more concerned about their chemistry test that morning or their cross-country meet or soccer game that afternoon. Here we were, barely a year after 9/11; why weren't they more willing to talk about the Middle East conflict and yesterday's suicide bombing? Perhaps I was still seeking some kind of closure for the loss of a former student in the second of the two World Trade Center towers to be hit. I thought about that bright, loving, generous young man who had been working for Cantor Fitzgerald at the time of the destruction and had left behind a young child and pregnant wife. Like so many others killed that day, this former student had held such potential to do good in a world sorely in need of it.

As the advisees left my classroom that morning, they were talking excitedly—about their games, about their social plans for the coming weekend, about their upcoming Thanksgiving vacations. I wondered what I could do, as a teacher, to make this bloody Middle East conflict come alive and get the attention of these high school students. I thought about the children growing up in the world and about what we could do differently to defuse violence more effectively and strengthen the foundations for more long-lasting peaceful coexistence. One thing stuck in my mind. During our discussion, when my students' attention had largely been waning, their interest was piqued when I asked them to voice their *personal* opinions about the continued construction of Israel's protective West Bank wall, about the failing health of Yasser Arafat and the growing importance of Mahmoud Abbas (or Abu Mazem) in the Palestinian world, or about the possible Israeli withdrawal from Gaza, beginning with the small Jewish settlement of Peat Sadeh. At this point, I noticed that several of my advisees spoke up with strong feelings about those issues, disagreeing with something another student had said. If only there were a way to keep this spirited intellectual surge going—and actually stoke it—rather than having it snuffed out by the sound of the bell ending homeroom period or an entire class period.

Nine months and almost one-half of a school year of planning and development later, the first Preventive Diplomacy and International Conflict Management and Prevention Workshop, focusing on the Middle East conflict, came to life in a conference hall five minutes from that library corridor where I had read the *New York Times* article that crisp November morning. The three-day workshop was filled with the incredible energy of fifty-five students and teachers, ready to tackle one complex issue: the Arab-Israeli conflict. The workshop would become the prime mover for hundreds of similar efforts I have engaged in since then as I founded the nonprofit organization Axis of Hope.

Axis of Hope's name is a response to President George W. Bush's second State of the Union address. In February 2002, the same year as the Jerusalem bus bombing, Bush had condemned certain countries—specifically Iran, Iraq, and North Korea—as being members of an "axis of evil." I was deeply disturbed by the ignorance it reflected, not just ignorance of the complexities of history, but of the impact of his categorization of these countries—his invitation to hate them. Following this speech and the president's "shock and awe" invasion of Iraq in March 2003—and the prolonged US military presence in that violent quagmire—it was of course the United States that earned the label "evil" in the eyes of much of the world. We would learn later of the deeply flawed US intelligence findings, astonishing ineptitude, and manipulative media packaging of the military response that allowed a president intent on launching an unprecedented preemptive military strike to have his way.

I felt at the moment that Bush uttered those three words—axis of evil—that we had to balance this perception of evil, of terrorism, of "others out to get us." We had to balance that with a self-confident, but not haughty, educational alliance—in the United States and abroad—to manage and prevent international conflict more effectively. And this had to begin in US classrooms where students in their formative years could learn so much more about how to prevent future conflicts like this. In the intervening ten years, Axis of Hope workshops have taught countless middle and high school students of diverse backgrounds about conflict management and prevention, with the goals of enlivening the imagination, awakening moral reasoning, and imparting lifelong social and civic skills.

"West is best" may sum up the history of geographic expansion in the United States, as well as its cultural orientation, what the French refer to as *chauvinism* or we might call *jingoism*. But times have changed, and so must our educational reactions. One thing I have found interesting in my conversations over the past decade with students, parents, teachers, and school administrators about the importance of global education is the catalyst of fear. Until recently, there were two commonly accepted human responses to fear—fight or flight. Yet both responses are ultimately self-defeating in a world where there's no room left to run and enough weapons to wipe out our species in one bad afternoon of nuclear one-upmanship. A recent scientific finding comes as timely and welcome news: among some of us, fear triggers a dramatically different response—an urge to prevent conflict and to engage in a new kind of preventive diplomacy with the reflex to, as Teresa Barker calls it, "tend and befriend." This suggests a logical direction for engaging people who seem most foreign and perhaps frightening to us sooner rather than later. It's time to head east, Columbus.

What Is Global Intelligence?

We can teach the next generation to break through historic patterns of destructive isolationism and militarism if we use intelligence not just as a military tool, but as an educational and cultural imperative for deepening mutual understanding and connection. We have greater resources than any generation in history—dynamic and creative teachers, cutting-edge technology and students who understand this technology, travel options (including local, national, and international), and funding sources—to meet the challenge of US isolationism. We can do better; and we must do it now. The dangers have never been greater and the stakes have never been higher.

I've developed what I call the global intelligence quotient, or global IQ, as an evaluation and strategic planning tool to identify the strengths and opportunities for improvement of a school's global education curriculum and improvement of the school community's GIQ as well. In a global IQ review, key categories and questions define the critical components of a strong curriculum for improved competence and global involvement and responsibility. In the pages ahead, when I refer to "boosting global IQ," I'm referring to ways to strengthen the content and effectiveness of a school's global focus as well as a personal or community perspective. It is an exciting process—for our students and ourselves.

The idea of global education in US K–12 schools is not new. In fact, terms such as "global education" and "world citizens" are increasingly commonplace in school mission statements, lists of core values, and curriculum discussions. A growing array of products and services respond to the expanding interest in global learning, including instructional software, books, games, curricula, study abroad, and educational travel programs. Most of us hear or see evidence of it in our schools, where colorful flags from different countries adorn the walls or hang from the ceilings in gymnasiums, auditoriums, and lunchrooms. Indeed, heightening awareness of other cultures is indeed part of most schools' basic philosophy and curriculum.

But this has not come without resistance and objections. One teacher, who taught in a classroom near mine for years, declared, "How can we think of all the global problems, and global responsibility, when we have so many problems occurring right here in the US or, in fact, right here in Boston?" An English teacher suggested that a global focus in middle and high schools would be premature; that it is the college years when students are able to learn to think globally—as he had done in college—not necessarily during their adolescent years.

Their comments echoed similar concerns and complaints I've heard voiced in parent and faculty meetings in public and private schools throughout the United States, from Boston to San Francisco, from Dallas to Detroit, and many points in between.

- What exactly is global intelligence and how, in addition to everything else, do we teach our students in order to raise GIQ?
- How will raising global intelligence affect students' performance in other subject areas? After all, doing their homework well in all classes, and turning it in on time is a very important part of their learning responsibility.
- Where is the funding for adding a new program like this? Our town, community, school board, or board of trustees might never approve this.

- What about students who already struggle with the demands of school? School is hard enough without asking more of them.
- With pressures on us to produce high scores on standardized tests, there's simply not enough time in the day to add something extra like this.

Any of these issues would be enough to end the conversation or postpone it if either were an option. But, as schools reevaluate their basic tenets, close to 90 percent are putting the words *international*, *global*, or *world* in their carefully crafted forty-five- to fifty-word mission statements or the core values displayed in bullet points on the home page of their websites. Imagine that you've just secured the copyright on your core values or your mission statement, and now your superintendent or head of school says that your educational approach has to reflect raising global intelligence—legitimately reflect it. The question is no longer whether improving a school's global IQ is feasible or can be comfortably accommodated. Now, the only remaining question is, how can I do so, quickly and effectively?

The Structure of This Book

Just as there are many ways to enrich a child's experience of the world, right in her or his classroom, there are many ways to enrich and expand the global education component of a school's curriculum, as well. However, I want to focus attention on what I consider five strategic changes—essential curriculum upgrades—that can transform a school's culture and curriculum in powerful, positive, lasting ways.

1. *Language and cultural fluency* (chapters 1 and 2): An initiative emphasizing early acquisition of a second language beginning in kindergarten, subsequent foreign language education in higher grades, and targeting an East-West balance. This includes the Eastern languages, Arabic and Mandarin Chinese, and the Latin-based Western languages, Spanish and French, in language and culture studies before high school graduation.

2. *Technology and media literacy* (chapter 3): An emphasis on integrating cutting-edge technology—computers, the Internet, teleconferencing, videoconferencing, Skype, and other communications tools, and the study of the news and social media—to expand learning and networking opportunities for students and educators internationally.

3. *Extracurricular activities and foreign travel* (chapter 4): Using the languages of the arts, athletics, and other extracurricular and curriculum-related endeavors to break down the walls between cultures, including education-based adventures on the local, national, and international levels, and hosting other cultures in our home communities.

4. *Case studies focused on conflict-resolution skills* (chapters 5, 6, and 7): Expanded case-study activities based on current events, providing content-rich, hands-on role-play experiences for students in the universal principles and practices of conflict management and prevention—the core curriculum of a new form of preventive diplomacy. I call this the "intellectual Outward Bound" experience and have developed specific case studies for use with students.

5. *Service learning and experiential education* (chapters 8 and 9): Allowing schools to develop community service or service learning in a way that stretches students' comfort zones, bringing them into contact with others in need and with their own vulnerability. This enhances their commitment to a universal code of compassion, while at the same time engaging all their senses—so crucial in their formative years. Involving parents and other community members can deepen the experience for all.

Although I have structured this book around these five objectives for the sake of clarity, in reality the effect of improving a school's global IQ occurs far more three-dimensionally. This means teaching our students (and ourselves) to think globally but to act in three other dimensions as well: locally, regionally, and nationally, with conscious attunement to the international context. Three-dimensional thinking can mean expanded collaborations among public, private, and parochial schools to bring students from all socioeconomic groups together for interest-based activities and workshops, service learning opportunities, athletic endeavors, community interaction, and international travel. It can mean expanded partnerships with business or philanthropic sponsors to bring funding to educational projects that enhance global learning experiences for all students and teachers. Or it can mean expanded professional development programs for teachers and administrators from public, private, and parochial schools, training them in cross-disciplinary, experiential pedagogical approaches to cultural literacy and conflict management and prevention skills.

These are not pie-in-the-sky ideas. As a nation, we have everything we need—the know-how, the resources, and the educational infrastructure—to make this happen. We have successful models: some progressive programs in global education are up and running in many of the nation's K–12 schools and school districts. Some parents have made global competency and citizenship a priority in their family's lives. We have brilliant, passionate educators, too: beyond the progressive models and the showcase programs is a nation of dedicated teachers, administrators, and other education leaders who are passionately invested in this work and in our children's future as global citizens.

We have money and other resources: models of public, private, and business support for important education initiatives are plentiful, no longer an educator's or parent's fantasy. Philanthropy underwrites progressive education programs around the United States and the world. There is a partnership possibility for every school in need, if we are willing to network and collaborate to help not only ourselves but others to find their matches. There are enough resources to go around, if we become advocates and activists for all, collaborators for the common good of *all* children, rather than only for our own children or school.

Finally, we have over 55 million children in our schools who are eager to start. Nature is on our side. Children are born hungry to learn, to grow, to feel mastery in the world, and to feel useful at every age. They are, as many teachers and parents recognize, like little sponges in terms of how much they can learn and how quickly they can learn. The developmental impetus has only to be fully engaged.

Our Children Come Hard-Wired for Global IQ

The great twentieth-century education and psychology theorists researched and wrote extensively about teaching global intelligence—without calling it that. While they did not have a unitary concept such as global IQ in mind, their ideas, still used extensively in US K–12 schools, offer renewed support for bold measures.

John Dewey, the American psychologist, philosopher, and educational reformer, championed the then-revolutionary idea of student-centered in-class experiences rather than the traditional memorization and regurgitation of facts more common in the first half of the 1900s when he was most active as a researcher and teacher. This led to the highly important idea of experiential education so familiar to us now. Jean Piaget, the Swiss developmental psychologist best known for his work refining the cognitive development theory into a series of four stages encompassing birth through adolescence, saw children as little philosophers, whom he called "young scientists building their own individual theories of knowledge." Using his own three children as experimental subjects, Piaget found that children were able not only to acquire foreign languages more effectively at a young age but to learn a great deal about other cultures and to refine intercultural problem-solving skills very well also.

Dr. Maria Montessori, best known for the theories and schools that she developed in an effort to improve education for poor children in her home country of Italy, crafted the Montessori method, based on carefully observing young children's learning characteristics and educational needs. She saw children as progressing through two stages of learning, in which they shared "universal characteristics" of learning, moving from an individually paced learning environment in their earliest years, to a more peer-oriented social environment for learning beginning at about age seven. Of particular relevance here is her belief that "all children are endowed with [the] capacity to 'absorb' culture," and if exposed to ideas early in life could learn them without feeling as if they were being taught. Montessori was also a firm believer in children's rights, in Italy and around the globe; in the value and importance of children's work so that they might develop themselves into socially conscious adults; and in the hope that this development would improve future students' conflict-resolution skills and lead to more widespread peace initiatives around the world.

Finally, Brazilian educator and theorist Paulo Freire espoused the "democracy of education." His work began with impoverished peasant youth in Brazil, whom he sought to teach so that they might overcome mid-twentieth-century oppression. Freire's *Pedagogy of the Oppressed* emphasizes the need to educate countries' native populations more effectively. Freire attacked what he called the "banking concept of education" in which the student is seen as a newly opened, empty bank account to be filled with a teacher's knowledge, rather than the student being an active learner. Freire also defended deep student-teacher reciprocity, in which students learn from teachers and vice versa. According to Freire, we should become teachers who learn, and learners who teach, because being much more democratic in our method of teaching is a basic foundation of modern education.

These classic theories provide a sound underpinning for progressive global education with the intention of improved global competency and responsibility. They are further supported by newer contributions to the field, including Howard Gardner's description of multiple intelligences and the defining quality of emotional intelligence that is so important for the interpersonal "people skills" of good leadership in any era, but more so in a time of deep and immediate global interconnectedness. What these theories describe, in essence, is how we can best help our children develop the intellectual flexibility, cross-cultural skills, and moral and ethical grounding to become responsible global citizens. It shouldn't surprise us that children are powerful actors in their own right, well before they get to college. In other societies, children are powerful actors, too. We know, for example, that Al Qaeda leaders have maintained training camps in Afghanistan, Pakistan, Iraq, Sudan, and Yemen to teach youth a radical version of Islam and train them to die fighting as young soldiers or as suicide bombers. We know that similar youth training goes on in Sri Lanka, Darfur, the West Bank, and the Gaza Strip and beyond. An estimated two hundred thousand to three hundred thousand children are soldiers for rebel or government forces in more than twenty countries, according to Human Rights Watch.

Whatever we call it—brainwashing, indoctrination, nationalism—when you strip away the politics, the religion, and the social and economic forces, what you have left is the powerful potential of youth to learn, act, and shape their world. If we want our children to grow up to make the world a safer, healthier, and more prosperous place for all the earth's inhabitants, then we must teach them how to do so, in new, more creative ways. The catch is that we can't really teach them in the same way as past generations educated children. Our parents assumed a somewhat more predictable world where the expectations of work, family, commerce, and politics followed traditional patterns. Today, we're painfully aware that all of these and many other social constructs as well as geopolitical developments are highly changeable and constantly evolving; creative, intelligent improvisation, beginning in the classroom, is the order of the day. It isn't enough to just read; our children need to be able to read *between the lines, and in different languages*. Why? So they can learn how to confront complex, often thorny issues and think profoundly and more effectively about solving these problems and, more importantly, preventing them from recurring. They need to be able to integrate ideas across disciplines and across cultures and be innovative, critical thinkers as they craft new collaborative responses to some of humankind's oldest sources of conflict.

Our young people are already out there—on iPhones, Skype, Facebook, surfing the Internet—forging friendships and accessing information and experiences, and sharing ideas and opinions about everything from movies and music to intimate details of their lives in online journals. Unlike any previous generation, they have the exciting real-time opportunity to interact, learn, and socialize with others worldwide, and they do so with an eagerness we often wish they would bring to conventional studies. How can we harness their love of interacting with peers, and this power and profound knowledge of technology, to their educational advantage? How can we, as teachers, administrators, parents, and students—or groups including all of these people—analyze what exists and then expand these opportunities to discuss current events, conditions, and circumstances more effectively? How can we allow more people to plug in and to connect with one another to prevent conflict more effectively?

These are the questions I and others have been asking for years. The answers fill a large and growing body of literature on progressive global education. Determined educators, parents, and policymakers (many but not nearly enough) have been persistent, eloquent voices advocating for meaningful global programs for our children. So I am far from a lonely voice in the wilderness. But I do have something to contribute from the nearly thirty years—thousands of hours—I have focused on learning exactly what global competency, literacy, responsibility, and citizenship really mean. And perhaps most importantly, I have investigated what students, educators, parents, and policymakers worldwide ask, need, and demand. While the hundreds of students I have taught over the years have worked to learn, I have learned what works for them—what makes them come alive with excitement for global studies and for meaningful action to resolve and prevent conflict. In my travels to schools in the United States and other countries, I have learned what students and educators are confronting and what they need to succeed. All that I have seen, heard, and experienced prompts me to say that we need to launch a national initiative for sound, swift educational change, and we need to do so as soon as possible.

I am not discussing a wholesale renovation of our curriculum here as much as a remodeling, taking what we are already doing well and adding to it a more globalized focus. All efforts, no matter how simple or sophisticated, have strengths that put them somewhere along an initiation-innovation curve. And no matter where you are on the curve, you can always initiate and innovate in some creative, collaborative way to advance the curriculum. Remember, as I so often say, "it is all about the kids."

My intention in writing this book is to encourage grassroots change, not to criticize or correct. I want to share an inspiring view of amazing teachers and young people that is currently missing from our discussions of them and their educational endeavors. I want to support foreign language study, to encourage collaboration with students in using technology in schools, to demystify the dynamics of conflict resolution, and to offer the principles of preventive diplomacy as a guide for charting your own course (or one for your school) in teaching global competence and improving your community's global IQ. Wherever you are in the process, I hope the stories here encourage you to take a step forward along the exciting path of supporting twenty-first-century global citizenship skills that these students are pioneering. As an educator, a parent, a public policymaker, or simply a concerned citizen, you need to show our children that it matters enough for you to take that step and the next one. However far it goes, it will be a step in the right direction. If it's a giant step, all the better. We have a lot of ground to cover and we need to move fast.

The Elements of Global IQ

Communication (in other languages)

Comprehension (of other languages and cultures)

Compromise (in conflicts created by difficulties in communication and comprehension)

Compassion (service to others)

Creativity (pursuing a new architecture of educational transformation)

PART ONE

FLUENCIES

CHAPTER ONE

The Argument for Starting with Romance Languages

Seventh graders, I remember, often didn't get much respect in the halls of Jefferson Junior High School in Minneapolis. But looking back, I can say that being a student there was a turning point in my life. My parents—Mom, the history teacher, and Dad, the industrial psychologist—had three boys: one in elementary school and two in junior high school. Both my younger brother, Will, then in fifth grade, and my older brother, Tom, then in ninth grade, had started showing real strength in sports: football, hockey, and baseball. I played all three, but didn't possess the same level of skill that they did. Where I did excel was in music—specifically, in piano, with a great music instructor, Mr. Cherwin—and in a foreign language, namely French. But I had no idea of the opportunity I was about to receive when my parents told my brothers and me that after the school year ended, we would be taking a trip abroad to France.

We were public school kids in Minneapolis. We didn't have a lot of money. But my father sat on the board of a local travel agency, and in exchange for attending the quarterly meetings the agency gave board members a choice: it either paid checks or gave an equivalent travel allowance. My dad chose to barter for five round-trip coach tickets to Paris. I tell you this because while finances can be a huge challenge to globalizing or internationalizing your educational experience—or that of your children—the solutions are often right at your fingertips, when you think outside the box.

Off we went that June, traveling on a modest budget, in what was to be a unique family bonding experience—two, fun, sometimes frantic, fast-paced, full-of-surprises weeks spent crisscrossing Paris and taking an overnight train to the south of France, tightly packed in a tiny train compartment. My parents believed children needed to take calculated risks in order to build self-confidence. Specifically, on this trip, we were to work on our knowledge of foreign languages and what I now call our "global street smarts." Before we had even departed on this family adventure, my father (a former professional football player and self-promoting family team captain) cheerfully assigned each of us certain plays or responsibilities for the trip. As if being in a huddle back in the 1950s while an All-American offensive tackle at the University of Minnesota, he smiled and said to me, "Since you're the one studying French, we're going to count on you to order our meals, get hotel rooms, buy train tickets. You're the translator for the trip. *D'accord?*"

At the time I thought it was a joke, maybe meant to humiliate me. Isn't that how seventh graders think? But Dad's much less obvious, more subtle idea was to improve my confidence, to get me to explore a path that could become my true passion, my true calling in life. My parents had been thrilled at the prospect of all of us learning foreign languages the old-fashioned way, immersed in the rote memorization and regurgitation of linguistic necessities of the Jefferson Junior High School French classroom. Yet when parents add the linguistic and cultural surround-sound effect, immersing their children during their formative years in the everyday life of another, totally different culture, the magic begins. This magic began that day I walked off the charter jet at Charles de Gaulle International Airport northeast of Paris, excited and nervous as hell.

What I have since learned from so many youth I have taught and traveled abroad with is that a tour of a foreign country—especially when you're young—can be a life-changing experience. That's what that first trip to France was for me. The trip is imprinted in my mind forever as one of the best times of my life. I will never forget coming out of the metro at Place Trocadéro and seeing the Eiffel Tower for the first time, just across the Seine. I will also never forget neglecting to remind my mom and dad to exchange money one Friday. With the banks closed on the weekend, no ATMs, few restaurants taking US credit cards then, and little money for meals, we found ourselves one

Sunday evening pondering how we would pay for dinner. I suggested singing some American or British songs on a street corner (my father and I were the only two in the whole family who could carry a tune) with a beret held out as our collection cup. My other idea was to go into a restaurant, ask for free food, and declare that we would do dishes in exchange for our meals. In the end, I convinced the manager of a small restaurant to let us eat nothing but *pommes frites* in his restaurant, because that was all we could afford. I don't remember my brothers or parents complaining about our meal of French fries, but I can still see the quizzical expression on the cook's face as he came out of the kitchen to see who was eating all those fries he was preparing, plate after plate after plate. It did not need translation.

I could not have played the role of translator on this trip, nor would I have embarked on a career with such a strong international relations component, had it not been for experiences like that first trip to Paris. I was also helped by some of the great teachers I had in my formative years. I will never forget Mademoiselle Brune (Miss Brown), my first French teacher, in seventh grade. Her passion for teaching the French language and culture to inner-city Minneapolis junior high school students infused me with a love of the language and culture of France. Her marvelous accent carried with it the flavor of the land that I fell in love with (and coincidentally reinforced the necessity of developing the best accent possible). Mlle. Brune would use one particular line with students who had not completed their homework assignments, something we *still* laugh about to this day: *Tu as été trop occupé pour terminer ton devoir hier soir? Ton cours de français est le cours le PLUS important dans ton école, en fait, dans ta vie!* ("You were too busy to finish your homework last night? Your French course is your most important course in the school, in fact, in life!") We tried to hold back our laughter, but found it impossible. She also spoke to us in French at all times in the halls of our school and had a lunch table once each week where we could speak the language for the carrot of extra credit.

I also remember Mr. Fred Oliver, my incredible French teacher from ninth through twelfth grades at Minneapolis West High School. He is a wonderful man in his eighties now—we still keep in touch—who was the essence of a stickler, not just in speaking the language all the time, but in having a perfect accent, excellent grammatical skills, and a deep treasure chest of French vocabulary and cultural lessons in the intellectual arsenal. He was what kids today would call "a pain in the butt." But as I have also learned, as a teacher myself for almost thirty years, a good pain-in-the-butt teacher who truly believes in your talents will mentor and push you so your language capabilities will be nearly perfect.

Mr. Oliver knew that most of the students at our school would never be able to travel to France, so he would take us on off-campus field trips to a moderately priced French restaurant where he would make us speak French while we ordered and ate our meals. Looking back, I realize that in these off-campus moments, on educational family vacations, and in school, using my very limited French abilities to experience new cultures and have the courage to immerse myself in what is considered foreign, I was not only learning French and about French culture, but experiencing the context of a larger world previously unknown to me. As I look back, the sometimes difficult or unsettling experience most often proved to be exhilarating, satisfying, and life changing.

Some twenty years after my father made me the family's rookie translator, I was hired as the founding director of a US boarding school's study-abroad program in Avignon, France. Each year, Proctor Academy, with its primary campus in Andover, New Hampshire, sent three groups of its French students, a maximum of ten students each trimester, to its Avignon-based program, which I founded in 1983, for a nine-week intensive program. I welcomed new arrivals from the United States with a task similar to the one my parents had given me. I met each group at the Paris airport, hugging all the fatigued, jet-lagged students as they emerged from French customs with their overloaded luggage. From there, we took taxis—three to a taxi, and the students had to tell the drivers where they were going—to the Paris Gare de Lyon train station where we would await the TGV train to Avignon, in southern France.

To the students' surprise, before we boarded our train to Avignon, I broke the group into smaller sections, handed one member of each 100 francs (this was well before the creation of the euro), and asked them to go as teams and buy different portions of the *pique-nique* we would enjoy together later on the train. The foods were available at an open market near the train station. Just as my parents had done years before, I forced the students—experiencing their first bout of language and culture shock—to do something by themselves. They had to take risks and use the language to achieve a goal, in this case purchasing our lunch for the train ride, but in a fun way and as a team. Each time, the students who arrived in Paris were nervous, but once they discovered that they could successfully achieve something simple like this, their fear began to fade, after only an hour or two in a new country. Yes, the students made inevitable linguistic faux pas, but they learned how to laugh and hop back into the conversation unafraid then, and for weeks to come.

These students taught me something early in my career as a foreign language teacher that made a profound difference in the way I understood foreign language acquisition. Many of the students who came to Proctor Academy had diagnosed learning differences (many were unfortunately labeled with having "learning disabilities"; I like to call them simply learning "differences"). For those, this diagnosis made traditional classroom learning difficult. However, immersed in the language and the culture of France, and forced to paddle along in French society, they were able to be successful over time. As Max, a student of Arabic we will meet in the next chapter, observes about the essence of learning a foreign language, "It isn't truly about textbooks or technology or teaching practices. Instead it is about immersion. This is when language acquisition works so well. I know students who had never taken a Spanish class and went to Spain for a whole academic year and were speaking with almost native fluency upon their return to the United States. They managed to do that without ever being asked to conjugate verbs or being quizzed on vocabulary in a US classroom."

To foreign language teachers, this realization might first occur with some discomfort. We want to believe that it is our language pedagogy that creates success, our curriculum that engenders fluency. But deep down we know that our students absorb information like a foreign language quickly and efficiently. If we, as parents and educators, commit to teaching foreign language in children's formative years, they will meet us more than halfway. Excellent foreign language pedagogy and acquisition are so important to improving a school's global IQ that I have devoted two chapters in this book to this basic idea. This chapter opens the discussion with the Romance or Latin-based languages where many of us began our language acquisition. Chapter 2 discusses broadening what we teach to include Eastern languages, Mandarin or Arabic, as well as Western languages, Spanish and French, in order to enhance the prospects of future peace and prosperity. In both cases, we must appreciate that our students are eager to match pace with their multilingual peers worldwide, and they are waiting for the opportunity to learn. What is the alternative?

Melting-Pot Nation Makes Savory Linguistic Stew

We know what doesn't work. Memorizing myths of Americana and encouraging what Dartmouth College educator and friend John Rassias called in 1964 "the moat mentality" of linguistic and cultural isolationism only put us at a deeper and potentially deadly disadvantage internationally. We have to use curricula in US schools to build bridges, not moats, and to give our children the knowledge and skills they need to maintain those bridges and to build more. We have to give them the tools to build cross-cultural relationships, tools they'll be able to use and adapt to meet future challenges and opportunities that we can only imagine today. We have to collaborate with one another—teacher to teacher, teacher to student, parent to teacher, parent to child—to prioritize creativity, critical thinking, problem solving, curiosity, imagination, and, especially, innovation in US language education.

The reputation of the United States as a monolingual society is in contrast to its reality as a nation of immigrants rich in foreign languages. Currently in our public schools, it is not uncommon for the English as a Second Language teacher to have children in class from two dozen or more different language backgrounds. Spanish, certainly. But also French, Mandarin and Cantonese Chinese, Tagalog (Filipino), Vietnamese, Korean, Russian, Polish, Italian, Greek, Hindi, Urdu, French Creole, Portuguese, and German. The United States can be described as traditionally chauvinistic in its adherence to English; not only do we consider foreign language instruction a low priority for younger school-age children, but we also pressure children from families that speak a foreign language at home to abandon that language as a sign of assimilation. And so often they do.

This divide is between de jure and de facto—between law and practice, between what we may want to believe and reality. Periodically there are xenophobic outbreaks of misplaced nationalism that seek to pass a federal law mandating English as the official language of the United States. We need only look at the local level, however, to see how such a proclamation would be at best counterproductive and at worst a veiled form of racism. It is a matter of our shared humanity that the California Department of Motor Vehicles publishes its documents in nine languages, including Armenian and Punjabi. New Mexico not only publishes all government forms in Spanish as well as English but also requires that all official services be available in both languages. Even Arizona, a state conflicted over the hot-button topic of immigration reform, requires the distribution of voting ballots in such languages as Navajo and Tohono O'odham—and Spanish—in certain counties.

English is the most spoken language in the United States. More than 82 percent of the US population speaks English as a native tongue, and more than 96 percent of Americans speak English "well" or "very well," as self-reported on the most recent census. Americans will most likely always feel that they must continue to teach children this "native tongue," given its importance around the world. But today's global culture, economy, and geopolitical dialogue demand more of those who want to shape the way Americans work and live. Bilingual fluency in Spanish and English is already a requirement for many jobs and careers. And it is not only an advantage in the workplace but also in community life where language differences have traditionally acted as barriers.

Latin-based Languages Are a Natural First Step

Spanish and French oral and written comprehension and expression skills are particularly well suited for integration into early education in the United States. These traditional Latin-based favorites offer young learners a natural step into foreign language acquisition. A young person who is bilingual in Spanish and English has access to a much wider range of work, study, and social interaction opportunities in the United States, where more than 35 million people, or roughly 12 percent of the population, speak Spanish at home (45 million people speak Spanish as a first or second language). Thus Spanish is the second-most-spoken language in the United States, and when compared to other countries where Spanish is spoken widely, the United States has the third-largest Spanish-speaking population of any country in the world, after Mexico and Colombia, and before Argentina and Spain.

The fact that Spanish is booming in the United States also means that for real-world language practice, students do not always have to travel internationally for an immersion experience. The important, long-standing, and profound presence of Latino cultures in the United States has provided ample opportunities for interface in this country. Spanish is, in in terms of oral comprehension and expression, relatively easy to learn. As I tell kids, with Spanish, what you see is what you get in terms of the consistent pronunciation of consonants and vowels.

I have taught both Spanish and French since 1983, so I am not playing favorites by outlining the national situation. Even as an avowed Francophile, I have had to contemplate the question, is French becoming passé? There was a time when French was the first choice of foreign language among many students. Some liked the elegant sound of it or its status as a language of great literature, cuisine, art, international diplomacy, and world leadership. Some liked the food—crêpe, croissant, quiche, café au lait—or other cultural appeals of France, including cinema, music, and architecture. Some just chose it because their parents told them to. In recent years, I've heard more debate on the merits of French versus Spanish, with the pro-Spanish argument (kids do actually argue over these matters) being that because it is America's obvious second language, it just makes sense to know it; that Spanish, too, speaks of a culture rich in literature and leadership; and that it is associated with good food that has long been underappreciated. I've also heard the argument that French isn't important in many places anymore.

Of course, that is not true, although French dominance as the lingua franca of international affairs and high culture has receded somewhat as other nations and other languages have grown stronger in the global milieu. However, the imprint of French history, culture, ideas, and the language itself is richly present in US history and culture. The United States' first two ambassadors to France were Benjamin Franklin and Thomas Jefferson, both fluent in French. Even in just a practical sense, what remains vitally important about French, absolutely undiminished by time or geopolitical shifts, is the same thing that makes any language important in the context of second-language acquisition: if you enjoy a language, for whatever reason that might be—from the sound of it, to why it might be useful to you, to whatever positive associations it holds for you—then it is the ideal language for you to study, in addition to English. And if you learn a second language well—be it French *or* Spanish—in your formative years, you have exercised a crucial area of the brain that will remain in shape and effectively usable for years: the oral and written comprehension and expression language portions of the brain. A student who has learned *how* to learn another language in those formative years will only find it easier to learn other languages later. For me, this was true as I studied and learned Spanish, after first learning English and then French. A good experience learning any foreign language trains the brain to acquire subsequent languages more effectively than monolingual brains acquire languages, and it opens the mind to the rich nuances of another culture's sights, smells, tastes, and surfaces, affecting all of the senses, a crucial exercise in multifaceted linguistic and cultural acquisition.

Foreign Language Learning Trains the Brain

Interestingly, it was prejudice and discrimination against children who spoke French as well as English that led the researchers Elizabeth Peal and Wallace Lambert to offer their watershed study on bilingualism and intelligence. Peal and Lambert found that not only did bilingual ten year olds in Montreal score higher on verbal intelligence tests than did their monolingual counterparts, but they also did better on nonverbal tests "involving concept formation or symbolic flexibility." Thus began a tidal wave of research that demonstrated how learning more than one language improves people's ability to solve problems, multitask, plan actions, and remember things. At the same time, other investigators debunked the assumptions made at the turn of the last century that a child who lives with two languages would have, in the words of Scottish educator and philosopher Simon Laurie, their "intellectual and spiritual growth . . . not thereby doubled but halved."

Suzanne Flynn, professor of foreign languages and linguistics at the Massachusetts Institute of Technology, believes the research is conclusive: there is no such thing as "finite brain space" where learning one language would mean that someone cannot simultaneously learn another. She points to studies in which babies as young as three months learn the difference between two languages, babbling slightly differently when they are with an English-speaking parent, for example, than when they are with their Spanish-speaking parent. "The child is differentiating these languages," Flynn says. "Children never get mixed up." Contrary to the belief that adding another language too early will interrupt or disrupt a learner's first or "home" language, "the capacity to learn languages is infinite," Flynn says. "It is only bounded by our time and our energy."

If a child can distinguish between languages even at three months old, can we draw the conclusion that the earlier a child learns a second language, the better? Flynn points to recent research by Canadian psychologist Ellen Bialystok, an expert on bilingualism and its effect on both cognitive development and language in children. This research indicates that language learning can continue into our seventies and eighties, and such language study may delay the onset of Alzheimer's disease symptoms. However, Flynn does agree that with respect to the sound of a foreign language, the earlier a student becomes familiar, the better.

This coincides with the conclusions of noted linguist Noam Chomsky, who asserts that very young students are able to perfect accents much more effectively than are post-adolescents, when intellectual pruning has taken place in the brain, making it more difficult to acquire a second language well, especially in oral expression. He also knows that infants are born with built-in syntactic or grammatical capabilities, or what he calls "universal grammar." What better time than during the kindergarten through eighth-grade years to learn a Latin-based language such as French, spoken in Louisiana (Creole) and Quebec, or Spanish, which is spoken widely and greatly influences the United States, from its use in foods to music to television and beyond? What better way to bring American youth together—particularly Latino and non-Latino youth—than by encouraging common bilingual and cultural understanding?

At the beginning of this chapter, I discussed the origins of my proficiency in one foreign language, but my case is not unusual. It would be even less unusual if we didn't wait until high school to begin teaching foreign languages to US students. Many have spent decades treating bilingual education as an example of appeasing the immigrant "have-nots" instead of recognizing that being bilingual or multilingual is an incredible asset for all students. The earlier a child learns a second language, the easier it is and the greater the future benefits. These benefits are not only cognitive; foreign language acquisition is also a powerful mechanism for change. Foreign language study stimulates brain growth that can enhance every aspect of a child's development, including social, emotional, moral, and spiritual development. The task of engaging what is foreign to us—words, sentence construction, ideas, and cultural perspectives, as well as the other senses, including the smells of unfamiliar foods, the sound of new music, or the sight of different colors or different art and material goods—literally changes the brain. It expands neurological interfaces, broadening and deepening the experience of the world and ourselves in it. A study led by Alexander Guiora noted that learning a second language—specifically with regard to pronunciation—requires an individual to take on a new identity; this learning anxiety in turn fosters learning empathy. At a psychological level, foreign language learning can foster emotional understanding rather than ignorance, self-confidence rather than insecurity, and healthy self-esteem in relation to others, rather than belligerence.

Ideally, foreign language acquisition should begin in kindergarten or early elementary school, followed by subsequent, more profound and challenging foreign language courses in middle and high school. "If education is a means by which to prepare children for the complicated world that they inhabit, to give them tools with which to understand new challenges, then the educational system should offer an expansive curriculum as early as possible," says Helena Curtain, former director of the English as a Second Language K–12 teacher-certification program at the University of Wisconsin-Milwaukee. Curtain is a respected author and international consultant in foreign language curriculum and teacher training. She continues, "Research has shown that through foreign language study, elementary school children receive the opportunity to expand their thinking, to acquire global awareness, to extend their understanding of language as a phenomenon, and to reach an advanced proficiency level in that foreign language. Parents, educators, and policymakers should find these reasons more than enough to prove the benefits of beginning foreign language study in the elementary school."

In *A Guide to Curriculum Planning in Foreign Language*, a State of Wisconsin publication, the following myriad short- and long-term benefits are attributed to acquiring foreign language proficiency early in life:

- One study found that it was much easier for students to learn other foreign languages once they had "learned how to learn" a second language in addition to English (for example, Spanish).
- Students developed a clearly enhanced knowledge of the history and geography of, for example, not only the Spanish-speaking nations they study in Spanish classes but the geography and history of other countries they became interested in as well.

- Many students who began to learn a second language in elementary school demonstrated higher SAT, SAT II, and ACT scores, especially in the verbal areas of these important examinations, than monolingual students.

These advantages—especially the last one—should interest all schools attempting to deal constructively with a variety of standardized test score obligations, which I turn to in the next section.

Obstacles and Challenges to Foreign Language Education

As a foreign language teacher, I can empathize with the obstacles of and challenges to beginning foreign language instruction early in a child's education. The school day is fixed: when you bring something new into the curriculum, you often need to cut something out. And this matters in human terms: if you cut a program, sometimes that means you cut a teacher as well. But as with everything I recommend in this book, I am not suggesting destruction and complete reconstruction of curricula. Rather I believe in remodeling our schools' curricula and, in doing so, overseeing an exciting, globally minded renaissance of US K–12 schools from within. And I believe in getting creative to do this.

Dr. Yu-Lan Lin, world languages program director in the Curriculum and Instruction Department of the Boston Public Schools, knows the "no changes, please" pressures of the assessment system in Massachusetts, the MCAS exam. She understands the way in which certain schools in her district have struggled to bring the English language arts and math scores students receive up from "needs improvement" to "proficient"—often doubling up on such classes, thereby reducing even further the hours available in the school day. She has also seen the desire in the communities that she serves; she has had hundreds of phone calls from elementary school parents requesting that their children begin learning a foreign language early on. But most importantly, she has seen some creative ways in which that language acquisition can begin in the formative years.

According to Yu-Lan:

> In the public schools, we are always under budget constraints. That is a given. It is up to the individual schools to use their own budgets judiciously. But when it comes to time, there are many methods [one can use] to schedule language learning creatively. Sometimes it is clustered, meaning that it might not meet every day, five times a week, but it can meet twice a week, along with other such "specialty classes" as art, music, and theater. We also have cases where the school offers language instruction outside of the school's hours—in their after-school programs, for example. When a parent cannot pick a child up at 1 p.m. or 2 p.m. because of their work obligations, we have been able to offer French, Spanish, and even Chinese in an environment that is at the same time structured and relaxed. The kids almost don't know they're learning—they just think they're having fun!

The ease with which these young students pick up the foreign language they are being taught, often by a parent of one of the school's students, is remarkable, but not unexpected. Research—and, of course, long, personal foreign language teaching experience—shows that young students are able to mimic their teacher well, picking up the teacher's accent and cadence. They lack the adult fear of making mistakes when speaking in a foreign tongue.

Unfortunately, historically and still true today, progressive foreign language opportunities that include early instruction and travel have been options only for progressive school districts like the Boston Public Schools or the affluent. Families with money, well-endowed private schools, and well-heeled school districts with enough resources for budgets beyond the basics provide this for their children. But, ironically, except for children enrolled in remedial English as a Second Language programs—children who lack English proficiency—second language acquisition has not been a meaningful option for most elementary and middle school children in the United States. Today, we have the opportunity to foster the most globally intelligent and adept generation in our nation's history, one that includes the rich and varied experience, creativity, and insight of a diverse population, beginning when children are in elementary schools, whether private, public, or parochial. We can build on that strength if we work collaboratively to network among these different types of schools to create synergy and to match funding resources—foundations, associations, corporate sponsors, and private donors—to expand opportunities for students from all socioeconomic circumstances. We can create, for example, service-learning programs similar to Jump Start, where bright high school and college students reach out to area elementary, middle, and high schools to offer free foreign language classes in exchange for high school or college credit, or simply as an important service-learning project. I am heartened by the prospect that our work to break down the international language barrier also can help break down barriers of socioeconomic class, beginning right in our own local areas, if we choose to work together.

Foreign Language Can No Longer Be Considered an "Elective"

Learning a foreign language during the elementary school years enhances not only cognitive development but also basic skills performance. As Marianne Fuchsen writes, "Foreign language study necessitates the acquisition of new learning strategies because it is foreign; basic to preparation for a changing world is the development of abilities to meet new challenges." The idea that the introduction of intellectual foreign matter or "foreignness" would lead to profound cognitive change in children was well known to Jean Piaget. He believed that when a child was faced with a word, a concept, an experience, or an idea that fell outside his or her realm of understanding, cognitive development—what I call "cognitive weightlifting" or "confronting cognitive conflict"—takes place. At this challenging level of learning, the brain's equivalent of weightlifting takes place, during which cognitive "muscle tissue" is exercised, broken down, and rebuilt over time, growing stronger. As we will see in part II of this book, Action Steps, such cognitive weightlifting becomes the catalyst for more effective cognitive conflict management or resolution. By that, I mean that this process forces neurons and synapses to develop a new multidimensional, multisensory, or, neurologically speaking, more global way of thinking, inside the brain. As Marcelo Suarez-Orozco, the Courtney Sale Ross University Professor of Globalization and Education at New York University (I love the title), recently reported in the *New York Times*, "Neuroscience is beginning to show that the brains of bilinguals may have advantages in what will matter most in the global era: managing complexity, rational planning and meta-cognition."

The evidence is conclusive. Foreign language acquisition is the closest thing to a global competency smart pill we can give our children in their formative years: fast acting and long lasting, with lifelong time-release benefits, proven effective and safe at any age (the younger the better), and with no negative side effects.

Some children may be fortunate because they hear languages other than English spoken at home or in the extended family. However, for the majority of US children, the only place or most logical place for them to learn a foreign language is at school. It is also interesting to note for comparison that students in France are required to study two foreign languages while still in grade school. If we are serious about preparing our children for success in the workplace—here or abroad—and assisting them *today* in leading lives as responsible, productive, contributing citizens in the global community tomorrow, then we must make foreign language acquisition a top priority in US schools. This is contrary to the current state of education, where according to a government-financed survey reported by Sam Dillon in the *New York Times* in 2010, thousands of US public schools have stopped teaching foreign languages in the past decade. The same report revealed that less than one-third of elementary schools in the United States offer foreign languages, while less than half of all middle and high school students are enrolled in such classes. We must make foreign language education a core subject in elementary, middle, and high schools across the country, as important as English, mathematics, social sciences, and sciences. If we do not, the United States will become increasingly isolated, vulnerable, and intellectually and creatively stagnant.

What We Can Do Now

- Start foreign language instruction early. And even if you can't add a class yet, then add content. Cover the classroom or hallway walls with reminders of foreign cultures, such as world maps; offer meals or even snacks that reflect international cuisines and other culinary traditions from other cultures; and collaborate with history or art department members on ideas that reflect foreign cultures, such as seeing movies about other cultures or visiting museums to learn about artists from other cultures. Look for creative ways to integrate foreign cultures across disciplines and around the school.
- Think *theater*. What kind of virtual reality language setting can you create with audio and visual elements? Songs in another language played on a computer or boom box, posters, videos, DVDs, newspaper clips, and language labels on everyday items in the classroom fill the spaces between focused learning activities and make the language an active part of students' learning environment.
- Enthusiasm is contagious, as well as instructive and perhaps inspiring. Show your love for another language. If you are a full-time or a part-time language instructor, or a volunteer parent who comes in after school twice a week to teach students a language, use the target language with your students all the time, both inside and outside the classroom, as Mademoiselle Brune did in my junior high school years ago.
- Lead by example. As a teacher or a parent, learn a first foreign language—or an additional foreign language—yourself. Research has shown that: (a) it is never too late to learn another language, and (b) the benefits of doing so are incredible (delaying the onset of symptoms related to Alzheimer's disease, for example). Being engaged as a learner also helps keep us humble, as we can empathize anew with the struggles of our students.
- Don't be afraid to play with the language. Years ago, Joe Troderman, a bright eighth-grade student in my second-year Spanish

class, invented a foreign language game, which has become one of my all-time favorites as I teach Spanish or French. Use someone's name to create an infinitive verb and then practice the conjugation of that name verb. Using his own name, for instance—Troderman—as the verb, he determined that it was the verb *trodermar* in the infinitive form. And then, using my Smart Board in front of the class, he asked, "How do you conjugate this newly invented verb?" He responded, smiling: "In the infinitive, it is *trodermar*, and conjugated it is *yo trodermo*, *tu trodermas*, *él/ella/Ud. troderma*, *nosotros/as trodermamos*, *vosotros/as trodermáis*, and *ellos/ellas/Uds. troderman*. This is creative, simple brilliance—and student-driven language pedagogy at its best.

- Invite students' initiatives and feedback, and get creative. Have them make family trees in the target language or plan their own restaurant and a marketing campaign to promote it, with menus in the language. Ask them to write poetry in the foreign language being studied reflecting the style of a particular poet they've been studying. Have them write an article for the school newspaper or website in the target language. Or suggest they develop a new product and produce an advertising campaign—including a filmed commercial—to sell this product.
- Collaborate with students concerning field trips, welcome them as consultants vis-à-vis their own education, and they will rise to the occasion as creative, constructive contributors. Examples: After-school initiatives, on or off campus, in the target culture's cuisine or cinema, or local field trips to museums, restaurants, and so on to increase socialization in the target language.
- Keep conventional testing to a minimum and aim for frequent short quizzes rather than long tests that cover more material than necessary and claim a full class period each week—or 20 percent of available instruction time. Have students work in teams to create a study guide for each end-of-term exam. Remember that their natural impetus is to want to learn and grow more competent and masterful.

- Language is social; keep it that way. Encourage students to form study groups outside class time. Assign collaborative projects and set up lunchtime tables for speaking Spanish or French.
- Global citizens are good for business, too. Share your vision and needs with local businesses and community organizations, and invite them to participate, for example, by financing students to have lunch in an area restaurant that reflects French- or Spanish-speaking culture. They may respond with cash support, with human resources—speakers or helpful advisers—or with instructional supplies of meeting space, food, transportation, or scholarships. Just *ask*—in the target language, of course.

CHAPTER TWO

Targeting an East-West Balance

Having students learn a foreign language isn't merely an academic memorize-and-regurgitate-information exercise. The net effect of this curricular initiative truly manifests itself when we and our students go beyond acquiring a working knowledge of or native fluency in one or more foreign languages. It is crucial that students study in depth, understand well, and appreciate and accept foreign *cultures*, including the racial, cultural, socioeconomic, political, and religious differences that exist in our fragile world. As American youth learn about other societies and other peoples in their classrooms, they learn to become what I call "linguistic and cultural chameleons"—in a positive sense—so that anywhere they travel, and with whomever they interact, they improve not only their understanding of the world but also our country's often tarnished reputation in the eyes of those who may dislike Americans. They can begin to help the country prevent conflict more effectively, too. Why? Because fluency in a foreign language enables one person to communicate directly with another person from another country, without the interface of a translator and without losing precious time and meaning. Not only does a willingness to work long and hard to acquire a language other than English communicate respect to people of other cultures, it also earns a student a measure of respect in return.

There are many cultures with which we in the United States have much interaction—positive or negative—in some cases to the point of social or economic friction and even war. Many people in these foreign cultures speak what the US State Department calls "critical languages," languages that more Americans should be learning and teaching to our youth as soon as possible. I am not against the Western canon; learning a language like Latin, for example, can be immensely useful as a foundation for the study of many Romance languages. Nor am I downplaying German or Russian, foreign language offerings especially popular following World War II and well into the 1980s. Any foreign language instruction is important to young people if it is offered early in life. I have already spoken about the inescapability of Spanish; I also believe there is still a place for French, German, Russian, and Italian, the most popular languages taught at the high school level in the United States. But in this chapter I discuss a meaningful East-West balance, along with these traditional foreign languages. Students need to understand the foreign languages that will be important in the future and which languages will dominate the twenty-first century, if we want the United States to succeed economically, diplomatically, and beyond.

First, schools must increase course offerings in grades K–12 in the language spoken by more people than any other tongue in the world: Mandarin Chinese. Second, they must also increase the availability of courses in the language spoken in countries at the center of the war on terrorism but which is seldom taught or studied in US K–12 schools: Arabic. Eventually more schools should also add limited courses in Hebrew, Farsi, Hindi, Korean, Punjabi, Turkish, and Urdu. And if language courses like these cannot be offered in the standard middle or high school curriculum, they could at least be offered as electives for advanced students, online or even as after-school programs.

I am heartened by the progress that has been made in some of the leading public, private, and parochial institutions regarding important, new foreign language course offerings. In much of the United States, however, we have a long way to go.

The Warning Shot of 9/11

Fear is a great motivator, but it has its limits. One of the aftershocks of the 9/11 terrorist attacks was the astonishing discovery that, although the US National Security Agency (NSA) had intercepted messages by Al Qaeda plotters several days before they carried out their attacks, the messages weren't translated until several days after the tragedies because of a shortage of NSA Arabic-language translators. Few, if any, of the freshmen starting high school that frightening September day in 2001 ever had the opportunity to study Arabic in school and to learn that in Arabic *al qaeda* does not mean terrorist; it means "base," "camp," "roots," or "foundation." More than a decade later, after involvement in wars in Iraq, Afghanistan (still ongoing), and Libya, and with China becoming a commanding player in global trade, little has changed. Fear and financial self-interest have had some trickle-down effect on foreign language education in the years since 9/11, especially reflected in the number of Mandarin Chinese programs that have sprouted up around the country. The National Security Language Initiative launched in 2006 by then President George W. Bush has also helped the United States oversee the creation of some critical language programs. And some K–12 schools, fortunate to have progressive administrators and faculty members and enhanced financial resources, have expanded their language offerings and taken significant steps to strengthen existing programs. But, unfortunately, most have not.

How scared or how concerned about the US economy, workforce, and security do we have to be before we take steps to bring the United States out of its linguistic—and often cultural—isolation? A friend who has survived three bouts with cancer observes with a certain fatalistic humor that after each diagnosis, and through physically and emotionally grueling treatment regimens, her motivation for living right—exercising, eating right, getting enough sleep—starts high but eventually, once she's feeling good again, fades away. She hates the idea that it takes a cancer diagnosis to get her attention and move her to action when she already knows what she needs to do. But so far, she concedes, evidence would suggest it takes a good scare. So it is for most of us and our nation: why should we "get in shape" with better foreign language programs? English is, after all, the most important language in the world, right?

Fear does get the adrenalin pumping for public policy initiatives, and given that China continues to rout the United States in the trade war, given that conflict continues in the Middle East and beyond, and given that experts say another terrorist attack on US soil is imminent, we can predict that periodic waves of fear will add urgency to the push for improved foreign language education. But we also know that fear is an imperfect motivator, which, as my friend indicated, can lose effectiveness over time. Fear freaks us out or wears us out. Fear does not, unfortunately, often lead to a sound, sustainable strategy for growth and improvement, whether we are talking about the economy or education.

Worst of all, fear isn't only an imperfect motivator; it is an obstacle, too. There is a palpable fear in this country of people who speak Arabic because many Americans automatically see the linguistic connection between the language and radical Islam or other Arab terrorists and, of course, the 9/11 attacks. The sound of someone speaking Arabic to a companion makes many non-Arabic speakers in the United States at least a little uncomfortable. Arabic speakers are subjected to suspicion and hostility on the ground and in the air, in a way unmatched with other Americans or visitors in recent history. (On my first flight after 9/11 from Boston to Buffalo, I was *very* concerned about a bearded gentleman sitting in front of me who resembled the images we'd all seen of Al Qaeda terrorists. Thanks to two Tylenol PMs taken with orange juice on the flight at 8:30 a.m., I was able to doze off and forget about my knee-jerk reaction.) Some also fear that teaching our children Arabic will introduce them to dangerous or violent ideologies—anti-American voices at the least—and that parents will be helpless to monitor the content of that instruction. Such hollow thinking has caused hysteria in parts of our nation to grow to absurd levels. In 2011, for example, a $1.3 million grant from the US Department of Education to the Mansfield, Texas, school system for the study of Arabic had to be returned by the district's superintendent, following an incredible negative outcry from parents and the community.

In a topsy-turvy world, fear can overshadow the fact that linguistic and cultural literacy is the best tool we have for defusing the power of ideologues and engaging other cultures—especially the Arab world—peacefully. If we are willing to step beyond fear as either a motivation or an obstacle—to "feel the fear and do it anyway," as author Susan Jeffers puts it in her book of the same name—there is a compelling conversation in favor of stepping up the pace of foreign language instruction. Language is the single most powerful tool we have for effective oral and written communication and positive change, from improved international relations to the lively dialogue between cells in your brain as you read this sentence. In the global realm, language is the foundation of communication and collaboration between peoples and cultures. It's how we convey respect for other cultures, too. Dialogue can draw people closer; it can ease tension and defuse hasty or hostile responses. There's a reason we refer to "talking someone through" a crisis. Language is power.

Starting a Mandarin Chinese Program

Of course, it is not always a level of xenophobia that obstructs the initiation of a program in an Eastern language. Sometimes progress is stalled by assumptions that the acquisition of Eastern languages is unnecessary because "English is still the international language" or "English is the language of business." Some objections raise familiar and understandable concerns, including budget constraints or lack of a suitable teacher. Other challenges are pedagogical: because the complexity of Eastern languages requires roughly four times the hours of study to achieve proficiency in languages like French or Spanish, according to one such argument, how can we expect to turn out fluent adult communicators quickly through the ordinary channels of middle school and high school? Then there are the popularly voiced concerns: "You are taking away important time from our students who need to focus on material in other disciplines, like English, math, or science." Another: "Hey, our report card as teachers is based on student results on standardized assessment or achievement tests. Offering a complex language like Mandarin Chinese or Arabic, which will take a great deal of time to learn, will negatively affect those scores—and negatively reflect on us."

But sometimes our resistance to necessary change—or what I call "educators in correction mode"—is exactly that: resistance. Good old-fashioned inertia, motivated in some cases by pettiness, reduces our national response to an urgent need for an eyedropper when the doctor ordered intravenous fluids. I have seen this up close when, as chair of the department of modern languages at a Boston-area independent school, I asked the head of school and the board of trustees if my department could initiate a Mandarin Chinese program. Now, sixteen years later, I am happy to report that the school's Chinese program has produced award-winning Chinese-language students and sent them to some of the best colleges and universities in the country to continue their study of the language than one could ever have imagined. There are more students taking Chinese than French or Spanish at this school, and it has recently hired a third full-time Mandarin teacher.

But I can still vividly remember the battle royale that ensued when I first suggested such a program at a faculty meeting, when one faculty member said, in a voice laced with a bit of anger, "We already have two modern languages being offered here—and languages should *not* dominate our curriculum!" When I asked what he meant, he responded: "(a) Why should we spread ourselves thin by offering a third modern language in your department, in addition to French and Spanish, a language that will not have many students taking it? (b) In terms of requiring a modern language, we require English. We require Latin. Why should we require a *third* language—like Mandarin—beginning in the seventh grade?" I will never forget his next sentence: "You're going to take a teacher who will most likely have only one class during the first year of the Mandarin program, with at most five students, and you are going to pay her as a half-time faculty member. And the next year she might only teach two classes. . . . Carl, are you crazy?"

My colleague's hesitation was exacerbated by the fact that it was going to take a tremendous investment of time and energy by a new teacher to, among other things, establish the curriculum for the class, obtain the necessary teaching materials, and build a program with trips to China that she or he led not only for students but also for parents and other faculty members. In the end, because of one forward-thinking head of school and one extremely supportive trustee, I finally received approval to establish this exciting program.

The board member, who had learned about the faculty meeting, supported the overall idea of improved globalization of the school's curriculum. (We didn't have the concept of raising a school's global IQ at the time, nor did we have a director of global affairs or other point person.) He was willing to provide preliminary funding to start a Mandarin Chinese program and to hire someone who had learned English herself as a second language—a very important skill, because she, more than a monolingual Chinese native, understood what American students would experience in acquiring a complicated second language.

After interviewing many good candidates, and just before boarding a plane for Changsha, Hunan, China, to adopt the oldest of my three daughters (Leah, now sixteen), one final candidate appeared on campus, and I knew after the first fifteen-minute discussion with her that this was the rock-star Chinese program creator I had been looking for. This wonderful, intelligent, creative, energetic, native Chinese woman who stepped up to our challenge of creating an excellent program is Jian "Jenny" Gao, arguably one of the best middle and high school Mandarin Chinese teachers in the country.

In a visit to Jenny's classes now, years after she was hired, you would not necessarily see the traces of stress and strain that we endured years ago when attempting to bring an excellent Mandarin Chinese program to Belmont Hill School. At 8:20 a.m., the first period of the day begins in the Mandarin Chinese classroom of *Gao lao shi* (teacher Gao). Soft, peaceful Chinese music is playing on a small, fire-truck-red Sony CD player perched on a shelf in the far corner of the classroom. Through the windows, the bucolic, green, grassy New England landscape offers a stark contrast to the Asian images on the walls. The large photographs are pictures of all Gao lao shi's current Chinese students, groups she has taken to the People's Republic of China (PRC) during two-week March vacations over the years, her Chinese class alumni who have continued their study of Mandarin in college and graduate school, and her students who are studying or have studied abroad through the School Year Abroad (SYA) program (see resources at end of book).

The walls of Gao lao shi's classroom are also covered with paper cuttings completed by her students. The intricate, colorful samples reflect students' self-expression through colors and patterns, an exercise in mental yoga, as Gao lao shi puts it, which prepares them in a hands-on manner for more effectively constructing in their minds the Chinese characters they are learning. The colors of the paper cuttings correspond to the colored, square pieces of paper on her whiteboard, on which many simplified traditional characters are written in magic marker. Other items placed around the room to enhance the linguistic and cultural setting in which the students are immersed for forty minutes each day include chopsticks, a small copy of an ancient Chinese terra cotta warrior, and an ornate Chinese sword. A box of small toys and puzzles, including a mah-jongg game, sits on a resource table near her desk. Gao lao shi uses these games at the beginning of each class, she explains, to make her students laugh, preparing their minds to be in a relaxed state so that they can learn the new, challenging language more effectively.

Even a non-Mandarin-speaking visitor to this class finds learning as natural as breathing. At one point, Gao lao shi solicits students' help in "teaching" something to the visitor—me—a foreign language instructor with *no* knowledge of Mandarin. A student explains that Chinese characters "are like pictures, or calligraphy." Gao lao shi comments, "Chinese characters are like this at first . . ." She throws a huge handful of chopsticks onto the floor, causing them to scatter all over in front of a semicircle of students' chairs. She continues, "Chinese characters may appear complex, as these chopsticks now appear, in disarray, but they are 'learnable,' and 'constructable,' and you will learn that as you put them together slowly and carefully, the characters will begin to have profound meanings, too. Watch, and you will begin to understand." I was pleasantly surprised that I actually did begin to understand, in this case how the expression "*ni hao*" (hello) appears in traditional Chinese characters.

Gao lao shi is a petite powerhouse of a teacher, with short-cropped black hair framing her wise eyes and ready smile. Her demeanor is extremely positive; she always smiles and listens well, too, a way of being that wins the allegiance of her students. They are willing to work hard for her. Gao lao shi's style is quick, interactive, and engaging, and she is generous with compliments to her students, too.

At one point, she looks a boy straight in the eyes and says, "Your accent indicates that you can speak almost like a native speaker." This is a bit of an exaggeration, yes, but a confidence builder for a thirteen-year-old boy in his first year of Chinese.

Gao lao shi embodies the kind of traits we can aspire to as teachers of any subject, but especially for those disciplines that are bound to seem so foreign to students. This type of excellent "mini-language immersion"—in this case, in Mandarin Chinese—is going on not only at Jenny's school. A few thousand miles away from this Boston-area classroom, a different beginners' class for young children is underway in Portland, Oregon. Here, the students all share the same qualities of engaged learners; they are energetic, enthusiastic, fearless, and willing to take risks while speaking the language and ham it up a bit when performing their dialogues in front of classmates.

Woodstock School in Portland is the home of the nation's first Mandarin Chinese immersion program for kindergarten through elementary school students, launched a decade and a half ago. Its graduates have moved on to study at the middle school, high school, and college levels, but return to Woodstock for the partial-day immersion program with the school's exceptional teacher. The "50-50 instructional model" program provides a half-day of Mandarin language study, the study of other subjects in Mandarin, and a half-day of the standard English language curriculum, largely so the students can meet state-mandated learning benchmarks. After a frantic, determined start-up was made possible by the serendipitous arrival of a gifted Mandarin language elementary teacher to the community, the program has been a remarkable success, says Cheryl Johnson, the former principal of Woodstock who launched the program and oversaw it for five years before her retirement. In terms of the children's response, the school's experience confirms all the research presented in the previous chapter about young children as open and able foreign language learners.

"The goal for the first year was for the children to be able to read, write, and speak 100 to 150 characters," considered an ambitious but reasonable goal, Cheryl says. "Every one of them passed. . . . Kids are much more resilient than we give them credit for, as long as they are engaged and excited about what they are doing. We often underestimate what they can do." With language and culture, she says, "we use more hands-on and visual aids and they pick up on it all that much faster."

During that time, the school identified several students in the class as warranting special education services, but did not automatically pull these students from the immersion class. "We didn't want it to be an 'elite' class—and we didn't accept the fact that special needs necessarily meant that a student couldn't be successful in this class. In the case of one particular boy, there was no reason to believe he would struggle any less in a standard classroom setting, and as it happened, the boy loved his Mandarin studies and was doing well in them despite his learning differences. Because it was a non-cognate language, for some reason it was easier for him," Cheryl says. "He was wonderful in it—and his parents said it was the only reason he wanted to come to school."

The program at Woodstock School has continued to grow and thrive, while dozens more Mandarin programs at every level of K–12 education have sprung up around the United States. In fact, enrollment in Mandarin Chinese classes nationwide has tripled in the past five years, accelerated by the post–Cultural Revolution economic, political, and diplomatic blossoming of the PRC. Just as Christopher Columbus, who was raised in the port town of Genoa, Italy, had an explorer's vision, so too do Gao lao shi and Cheryl Johnson and other visionaries who have gone on to found excellent Mandarin programs in US K–12 schools.

I am inspired by the spirit demonstrated by these explorers—these risk takers—from our and other cultures. I like to think we might encourage our K–12 students to adopt that "international explorer" mentality also, motivated by the prospect of advancing something very simple: better communication and more peaceful coexistence in our rapidly shrinking, increasingly interconnected world.

Starting an Arabic Program

Another such "explorer," in his case in Arabic, is a young man I got to know at Boston University. And he is my hero in starting an Arabic program at the high school level. His name is Steven Berbeco. What he has done at Boston's Charlestown High School is amazing. Charlestown High School is an urban public school, with all of the challenges that such a description might conjure up: high absenteeism, low performance on the Massachusetts state MCAS exam, a relatively low graduation rate, and overcrowding that causes scheduling chaos. It was the center of often-bloody resistance to Boston's court-mandated busing in the 1970s, too. But Steven showed the kind of innovation that was necessary to improve this school's global IQ, remodeling rather than destructing and reconstructing one of the school's curricular offerings. Steven had been hired to establish an Arabic program at the school. At first, he had very few takers. Then he noticed that a number of students had the same free time in their schedules. The plan had been to put them all in the Junior ROTC program, regardless of their interest in it. He made these students a deal: during this time, they would not have to go to ROTC. Instead he would start teaching them Arabic. But if they gave him any trouble, they wouldn't be headed for detention; rather, he would close down the entire program and they would be placed in the Junior ROTC program.

The students agreed and found that they loved the challenge of learning Arabic. Steven noticed what we all have seen on our best days as teachers: students will take on a challenge when it makes them look and feel special. The shrewder ones also pursued the study of Arabic because of how it would look on their college applications, and because they felt that this language might help them when applying for jobs one day. Arabic is, after all, the sixth most commonly spoken language in the world, after Mandarin, English, Hindu, Spanish, and Russian, and it is likely to be equally ranked with or to pass English by 2050.

In addition to the well-documented, widespread problems of inadequate competency in Arabic I referenced earlier, there is another form of US intelligence failure, namely, how we fail to effectively educate intelligent Americans about the Arab world. How can we teach our children to engage in constructive Arabic dialogue and interaction with peoples in other parts of the world, instead of instilling them with the fear, mistrust, and hostility that currently dominate discussions and that are exacerbated by US reliance on oil from the Middle East? When will we learn that widespread addiction to such video games as "Call of Duty: Modern Warfare 3" only worsens our hatred and mistrust of others, especially those in the supposedly terrorist-filled Arab world? The answers to these questions, and what classes like Steven's demonstrate, lie in exposure to the language spoken by 250 million people worldwide.

Steven tells some amusing stories about students showing off by doodling their names in Arabic on their desks in other classes, so that the teachers in those subjects have to ask Steven who has been committing the infraction. But he tells deeper and richer stories, too, about a student who overhears a cashier speaking Arabic in her local Walmart and strikes up a conversation with him. Or a student who sees someone reading an Arabic newspaper on the subway and talks to that person about not only the headline but also the way the story is reported in the Arab media compared to the Western media, and Steven's students remind me that. I once met a young man from Newton, Massachusetts, who was learning Arabic as well as Hebrew. He came from a devoutly Jewish family, and his mother and father were completely supportive and excited that he was engaged in the study of both languages. His goal was to be, in his words, "a cool Jew, one who didn't need a translator to get around in the Middle East, and who could understand multiple sides of political issues, more from the inside out." What a refreshing perspective! Instead of coming into potentially fraught situations and saying, "You know what? You need to learn our language, English. Sorry, but that's the way it's going to be," this student felt the fear and took the challenge anyway: he has begun to respect another language and culture—namely, Arabic—and to study it with the goal of becoming fluent. He and Steven's students demonstrate crucial reflective skills that I return to later in this book, when I discuss the importance of teaching students media literacy.

The Charlestown school administration, community, and parents have supported and encouraged the study of Arabic in Charlestown High School, unlike the xenophobia shown by residents in places like Mansfield, Texas. Steven and the town's school board have utilized a federal grant to not only develop the academic year program into three levels of language learning but also introduce the Arabic Summer Academy at Charlestown High school, a five-week intensive program for sixty Boston-area public and private high school students that offers the equivalent of a full year of high school Arabic. The program is free: all of the course materials, backpacks and other donated items, and breakfast and lunch are free. Students are even paid a $500 "severance" when they finish the program to partly compensate them for the earnings they have missed by not having a summer job. Many students have commented that not only does their knowledge of the Arabic language and culture increase exponentially during the Arabic Summer Academy, but that it is also the first time they have studied alongside students from private, public, and parochial high schools. This is an excellent example of communication, collaboration, creativity, and coexistence—key pillars of the kind of preventive diplomacy I first referenced in the introduction and to which I will return in chapter 5.

There are challenges within the Arabic Summer Academy at Charlestown High School, of course. Finding teachers who have the right kind of training is the first. Teacher training was for this reason the focus of Steven's work during his most recent sabbatical. While there may be many local native speakers with linguistic competence, they might not have the required pedagogical competence to be effective instructors in the program.

Another challenge is the curriculum. Steven estimates that 95 percent of the nation's Arabic students use a text published by Georgetown University Press. (Throughout the textbook is the narrative of a particular woman. The joke is that any two people who have been studying Arabic anywhere in the world can get together and discuss this woman's problems as an introduction to one another.) The curriculum, we have learned, is also better suited to collegiate learners than those at the high school level. (As of 2011, there has been exactly one high school curriculum for Arabic study published in the United States, and there is virtually no effective curriculum for those wishing to teach Arabic to middle school students or younger.)

An additional challenge Steven cites is the lack of organized associations of Arabic teachers in the United States where educators can share best practices; exchange materials and planning tips; receive troubleshooting support from their colleagues; and generally enjoy the legitimacy that such an organization can give to a new field. Fortunately for Steven and others, the New England Association of Arabic Teachers, which is in its relative infancy, is nearby. Another growing organization is the American Association of Teachers of Arabic (AATA), based in Birmingham, Alabama (http://www.aataweb.org).

Ahlan wa salan, Josh (Welcome, Josh)

While I have been exposed to programs like the Arabic Summer Academy and the Middlebury-Monterey Language Academy, I have met many young people who are examples of students who attend schools with good global IQ (see the resources at the end of the book).

One example of a young man who took the challenge is Josh, now age twenty-one. At sixteen, Josh didn't think of himself as an articulate activist for progressive public education, having spent much of his time strategizing how to get out of his schooling. A bright young man, he was nonetheless a difficult student. "Let's face it, I was a pain in the ass," he said, looking back on several miserable public and independent school years. After moving to the Freeport public middle and high schools, near Portland, Maine, he was still trying to get out of school, but for better reasons than behavior problems. Having completed his core requirements for high school graduation, he applied to complete his high school career (and receive a diploma) studying abroad, on an American Foreign Service (AFS) program in Turkey. While studying there, Josh hoped to move quickly into college-level studies in international relations, with a specific interest in coexistence work. The reason for this: several years before, he had had an incredible three-week summer experience at the Seeds of Peace International Camp in Otisfield, Maine. There he got to know Palestinian and Israeli peers very well. He learned of their plights in the Middle East. He learned that *they* were multilingual and multicultural. And he wanted to be so too. Although he understood why his school didn't, and still doesn't, offer Arabic—"They had to do a lot and they don't have the money"—he didn't want to bide his time in conventional US core class offerings for another year. He was ready to move on. "Brain scientists say that the capacity for delayed gratification doesn't kick in 'til you're twenty-five, so I'd say I'm normal," Josh says. "I didn't want to wait."

Josh had always had a lot of intellectual energy, much of which ran contrary to conventional demands in his early years. Some early speech problems—"I couldn't say most consonants, and no one could understand me, so I was frustrated a lot of the time"—made matters worse. Starting out in a private school with a modest early foreign language acquisition program, Josh took Spanish once a week from second through fifth grades. During this time, his speech issues began to resolve—with the help of a school speech therapist—and his Spanish continued to progress. "I had an ear for it," he says, but he didn't have the patience for a class he found mind-numbingly boring in seventh grade. Adolescents don't always say things tactfully, but they tell their own truth. As Josh explains, "in eighth grade, I switched to French because I hated the Spanish teacher, and the French teacher was nice and you got to eat a lot in the class."

The summer of eighth grade was a turning point for Josh, when he attended the Seeds of Peace camp. Most of the international students, teens like himself in many ways, opened his eyes to the stark differences in their lives. They were conversant in at least one other language in addition to their native Arabic or Hebrew—and most either spoke some English or spoke it very well—while the American students, like Josh, were limited to communication in English only.

Meeting the international students for the first time and experiencing the friendships that followed channeled Josh's curiosity and energy into the global arena: "I was in awe, not only at what they'd been through but also that there are teenagers who are serious and care about the world—like me. As an American, you can't compete with the emotional background they come from. For most of us in the United States, the question is 'Where were you on 9/11?' They talk about walking home from school and their sister not coming home because she's been killed."

Josh has since stayed in touch with his new friends on the Internet, through Facebook, and through e-mail and instant messaging, benefiting from the all-important use of technology I will explore in the next chapter. But he also recognizes that the camp and Internet dialogue that the international teens enjoyed was, in a sense, an "artificial construct." "In the real world," Josh says, "you would never have all these nationalities getting along—you'd never have them in the same place, in the same room, coexisting peacefully. So it's more like an individual relationship you have with each one, and a network of us all."

However foreign relations in the real world have historically incorporated distance and distrust, the networking that Josh describes, made possible at this summer camp, is a glimpse of the new terrain for improved global citizenship and better US diplomatic training, beginning when US students are in middle or high school. This is the new frontier, and he and his peers are truly pioneers. The difference for Josh and his colleagues is that, having seen the consequences of the conquest mentality, they are focused instead on actively engaging in collaboration and the work of coexistence. Josh's experience may not yet be widespread, but no longer can he and others like him be considered outliers. Many students recognize the need for a truly global education. They may not be consciously engaging with this learning for security or trade reasons, but they do understand that they have much to learn from—and about—the Arab and Israeli cultures, as well as the traditional West. As teachers, we must encourage their curiosity to explore the entire world with a passion that such exploration is worthy of.

What We Can Do Now: A Buffet of Creative Suggestions

- Focus on one foreign language—Spanish, French, Mandarin, Arabic—early in students' lives and teach it well, allowing them to learn how to learn another language well, before studying a third language, after English and the first foreign language.

- In formulating school offerings, aim for a balance between Eastern and Western languages.
- Think creatively. Use community resources for an immersion experience: foreign language and culture-related activities in the area where your school is located, like taking students to a Chinese restaurant or an outdoor market where Arabic is spoken; having guest speakers who come to talk in the target language and about other cultures; taking field trips to museums that reflect the culture you are teaching; overseeing fun, creative "Foreign Language Day" show-and-tell activities within your own school or with other schools.
- Tap the local colleges and universities for those fluent in the foreign languages you offer, or would like to offer. If your school does not currently offer Arabic, for example, and you are a Spanish teacher, consider having a graduate student or professor of Arabic come in for a unit to discuss the relationship between the two cultures and languages, and how many Spanish words actually come from Arabic language (*alfombra*, *almacén*, *algodón*, etc.).
- Support the search for and hiring of two important kinds of language teachers: native speakers who have had to learn English as a second language, thus enhancing their empathy for those struggling to learn a language very different from their native tongue; and Americans who have learned the target language well and as their second language. Students benefit tremendously from seeing the process of language acquisition when their courses are offered from these two kinds of excellent, passionate teachers—like Jian Gao and Steven Berbeco. This is what I call the "zigzag" team approach to foreign language pedagogy.
- Not all exposure to foreign cultures has to come from the study of foreign languages. We need to look beyond American and European history and include such subjects in our K–12 curricula as a study of Chinese history (the Ming Dynasty, Mao

Zedong, etc.), the Koran, the Ottoman Empire, the history of the Taliban and Al Qaeda, and Islamic fundamentalism, all in very basic, easy-to-understand ways.

- Create a Global Issues course: The study of current events, in the target language, if possible, and reading and discussing articles in an international newspaper each day will allow students to learn about current geopolitical conflicts. It also offers an intriguing subject for students that enhances cross-cultural understanding.

CHAPTER THREE

Establish Learning Goals First; Harness Technology Second

From snail mail to faxing to Skype, from blackboard to whiteboard to Smart Board, and from landline telephone to 2G mobile phone to BlackBerry and iPhone, we have come a long way. We live in an exciting era of engagement, communication, and transformation—fueled at every turn by technology. With this new technology are new expectations: live discourse both inside and outside the classroom has sped up, for example. And while some dangers associated with the new technology bear discussion (Is too much of it just games? Is its true value in programs like Rosetta Stone over live language instruction?), I think the myriad, original, innovative possibilities far outweigh the obstacles. It's true that you don't have to have a keyboard or an Internet connection to explore the world, learn about it, or enjoy it. But technology has redefined the world in so many fundamental ways that our children's experience of technology—being surrounded by it, immersed in it, living in it, learning about it, and traveling around constantly using it—is inherently different and in so many ways richer than before.

This chapter is about the effect that technology can have on improving your school's global IQ. How? By enhancing "media literacy"; by allowing students to practice and improve the negotiation skills that are so instrumental in preventive diplomacy; by using virtual reality to connect them with peers in schools several blocks or thousands of miles away; by creating more peaceful international friendships in the end; and by expanding learning opportunities for students and educators, while retaining the delicate balance of educational challenge and play.

But global engagement isn't something you can just order up in a classroom or drop in from a computer connected to an LCD that displays images on a screen. Even with the most sophisticated technology, meaningful student engagement emerges from true curiosity about other languages, cultures, peoples, and customs. And it requires the courage of students, teachers, administrators, school board members, and parents to take some risks and venture into new territory together. What stands in the way is "the educational cocoon"—an intellectual comfort zone. In my experience, negativity toward technology in education is circumstantial. Ignorance hobbles us; improved knowledge sets us free. We demand that students learn how to think new thoughts and do new things, even though the process may make them feel hopelessly incompetent at first. We must be prepared, as teachers, to do the same. The first step is to place educators, administrators, and students in more carefully constructed, creatively thought-out, technologically enhanced global settings, right in our own schools. Beyond rote memorization of foreign language vocabulary and conjugated verbs, this includes finding new ways to bring other countries, languages, and cultures into our classrooms—something that can provide students with a virtual experience that will then lead them more effectively into understanding and learning from the real thing. And we can achieve so much of this through technology.

We have the greatest boon to globalization right at our fingertips: computer-linked projectors, wireless laptops with built-in video cameras, individual course websites, e-mail communication between students and teachers, Internet research and rules about it, even distance learning programs that allow students and teachers anywhere on earth to "show up for class" at the same moment or at different times of day, thousands of miles apart. Such bleeding-edge technology has become increasingly affordable and accessible, though not all of it needs to be deployed in every situation, as I will explore later in this chapter. As Boston Public Schools Director of World Languages Yu-Lan Lin mentioned in chapter 1, there are "always . . . budget constraints; that is a given." Indeed. But I wonder if sometimes we don't cite many of those budget restraints to disguise our own fear of change, in this case our concern that we, as adults, are no longer in our formative years of life and will not be able to develop fluency in these new technologies. My response to this predicament (and this from a teacher who has experimented with a lot of technologies, rarely successfully at first) is "to feel the fear and do it anyway." Our kids and their futures depend on it.

What Is Technology?

In this book, I define educational technology as nothing more or less than a mechanism—such as a computer, an LCD projector, or a cellphone—by which learning is enhanced, either as a conduit through which information is delivered or connections within or outside a community are created more quickly and efficiently. Technology as a tool to enhance education can be as simple as creating a new classroom configuration, like the Harkness tables that became prominent in the 1930s. Named for education philanthropist Edward Harkness, the original Harkness table was an expansive, oval conference table around which students gathered for class to discuss issues, ideas, or lessons, rather than sitting at desks in a grid pattern in the classroom listening to the teacher and then memorizing the material to regurgitate later. When I was starting out as a foreign language teacher, my school couldn't afford the name-brand Harkness table. I decided that it didn't matter; students and I placed four square tables together to make a bigger square. Although it barely fit in my room, the effect was the same: discussion-based learning, every minute of every class, every day. (Student desks or chairs can be placed in a circle or oval to get nearly the same effect.)

As Harkness himself said in his will, "What I have in mind is [a classroom] where [students] could sit around a table with a teacher who would talk with them and instruct them by a sort of tutorial or conference method, where [each student] would feel encouraged to speak up. This would be a real revolution in methods." Well, more than eighty years have passed, but "Harkness education," as the student-centered interactive discourse method is called, remains a viable, vibrant, and in many cases, revolutionary pedagogy. Teachers lob ideas into the middle of the table and watch as the subject matter catches fire during discussions, while pedagogical goals such as memorization or regurgitation are marginalized. Wonderful democratization takes place between the shyest and the most gregarious students, as well.

Your intended use of technology all depends on your intent for a particular course curriculum or thematic unit. Or, in the words of old friend and former colleague Dr. John Thurner, for years an independent school director of technology (the same school at which I was chair of the department of modern languages in the early 1990s): "Establish learning goals first, technology second."

In those early days of computers, John had his hands full with me and some of the other gadget-nerd teachers and students at our Boston-area school. John was greeted on his first day on the job by teachers such as me tapping on his door, asking him to share his advice about a list of hardware items that we then wanted to order to enhance our courses.

During that exciting—but in a way overwhelming—time, I had visions of everything that computers, the latest software, and the Internet could do for my students very typical of my "full-plate" personality. I'd been reading up on everything and wanted to do it all. John was cheerful but circumspect when I handed him my list. He handed me a homework assignment: go back and define the outcomes, the goals of the enhancements I had imagined that technology would deliver. Once I could reflect on what I and the modern language department wanted to achieve educationally, he told me, he would be able to help me assemble a technology plan—including hardware and software support—to advance that goal.

I hadn't thought of it that way, nor had many in my school or in many other schools for that matter. At that point—in what might be called the "before" years—every surface (floors, walls, and ceiling) of my ancient classroom was cluttered with international maps, posters, signs, and other foreign language paraphernalia, basically, lots and lots of paper. But in the back left corner of my classroom was a large, rather bulky wooden rolltop desk, a brown eyesore to the casual observer, but not to me and to my students. Inside the desk was my first computer, an old Power Mac, which I still keep in my home's "educational museum" to this day. Why did I have this monstrosity in the back corner of my classroom, impeding students' passage around the table and blocking the light from the windows behind it? Because I was convinced that technology as it applied to enhancing education was here to stay and that students had to be able to experience the language and the culture of other lands through a virtual exploration, right there in the comfort of their own French or Spanish classrooms.

We would laugh at that computer today, imprisoned in its huge "computer camper on wheels," with its floppy disks and small microphone just above the screen where students and I could record our voices into an internal recording device. I asked John if I could have an AOL account (having just read about AOL), not to surf the web, but to create an e-mail password—Loire—and to contact regularly other teachers in French- and Spanish-speaking countries. Why? In order to see if even one might be interested in setting up an e-mail pen-pal program with my French and/or Spanish students, instead of the more traditional snail-mail pen-pal programs that had existed for years prior to this. After weeks of not hearing from any teachers living and working in another country, one afternoon, during a regularly held middle school extra-help session in my classroom, I heard the computer go "bleep." The students and I were excited to find that I had received an e-mail from Ghislaine Boivigny, an English teacher at Paris's famed Lycée Louis-le-Grand (graduates include Molière, Victor Hugo, Lafayette, Baudelaire, Delacroix, Degas, Pompidou, Chirac, Citroën, and Michelin, to name but a few), stating that she would love to participate in an e-mail pen-pal program between my American students studying French and her French students studying English.

Ghislaine—who is still a dear friend to this day whom I visit when in Paris—and I, in a pen-pal test exercise, decided to combine language and culture studies by asking each group of students to work together and write the class across the Atlantic a letter describing the image(s) they had of the other's culture and everyday life. The recipient class (because my students wrote first, this was the Lycée Louis-le-Grand students) would then respond with (courteous!) corrections of grammar and misimpressions of their culture, and add a round of preconceived notions they held about US culture in English.

The first letter sent by my intermediate French students, as an attached document in Microsoft Word, used French grammar that was not perfect, and declared—in detail—that French people loved to eat frog's legs, wore berets, and traveled everywhere by bicycle with a loaf of French bread in a bag on their backs! In response and after correcting these preconceived notions, the French students declared that most Americans must watch football on television each day, sitting in La-Z-Boy chairs, eating bags of potato chips and drinking can after can of beer! The instantaneous responses, taking in some cases only a few hours, added to the excitement of the educational—and-fun—exchanges between my class and Ghislaine's.

Advances in computer technology and communications have in some ways made those early e-mails almost as quaint as the snail-mail letters of a generation earlier. But the goal was and remains the same: use whatever small, creative ideas you can to enhance your students' global IQ through the acquisition of foreign language skills and the development of cultural fluency—accompanied by an evolving fluency in technology, wrapped in a fun exercise involving peers living thousands of miles apart.

My friend John Thurner was right: once you are clear on the benefit or learning outcome that you want to accomplish—in this case, connecting students so that they can help one another learn more effectively about a foreign language and culture—you can then discern the plan and the pieces to accomplish this outcome. The students themselves often upgraded our effort through their own creative applications. One student, Steve, taught me how to use PowerPoint as an integral tool in teaching my French and Spanish students about the cities their e-mail pen pals lived in, rather than simply giving an oral presentation, well before this became a widely used pedagogical tool. Out with my old, dusty overhead projector! His lessons still resonate with me whenever I give a lecture using PowerPoint when I am teaching at Boston University.

To use technology in the best and the brightest ways, we need to set aside the old clouded lenses and see its powerful possibilities in the classroom in new ways. We need to see students through a fresh lens as well, recognizing that at times they may be some of our best technology allies, or our best teachers. They are typically way ahead of us in technological savvy—and in openness to learning—possessing an intuitive comfort level with computers, software, and innovative usage of these tools. And regardless of their level of technical experience or expertise, students are always valuable consultants on their own education as well. Why? Because they can show us what's exciting for them in the technological array and what works as an effective tool for enhancing teaching and learning. In teaching us, they are learning to teach. If and when we give them credit for knowing more than we do, if and when we are humble enough to admit that at times they can be our smart, involved, understandable—and understanding—teachers and mentors, their willingness to learn lessons from us, as a team, improves significantly.

Technology can help us to see not only the world in new ways but also our students in new ways. One former student, Ryan, was only a junior in high school when he helped me to create the first Axis of Hope website. His interest in and knowledge of technology—and his ability to create nifty websites—absolutely amazed me. He had a natural ear for French and was a fairly good student. He also had a distinct interest in studying French and eventually traveling to France—help with the latter I felt I could offer him in exchange for his invaluable assistance with technology in my classes, and as I was establishing Axis of Hope.

But Ryan's true interest in French went beyond the classroom. For Ryan, the idea of communication with his classmates, when they were confined in my classroom, was just OK. But e-mail communication with students in France was an even better way for him to practice and improve his language skills, learn about another culture, and meet and befriend—via cyberspace—one or more students. And he hoped to meet them face-to-face, thanks to technology in the classroom or in his suburban Boston home, or by actually traveling to France.

What happened next was memorable. One Parisian student, a Lycée Louis-le-Grand junior, whose family lived on a barge on the Seine near Notre Dame Cathedral, began communicating via e-mail with Ryan. He shared his interest in the Internet and in helping adults create websites. This was just what Ryan was looking for: a student who shared his interest in the Internet. Ryan asked me if he could discuss visiting Paris and his new online Parisian friend. I agreed, so they chatted—online, of course, and many, many times—about whether they could see one another the following summer, and Ryan was thrilled to be able to stay with the boy and his family on their barge on the Seine at the time. Was it the intermediate French class e-mail pen-pal activity that got Ryan started on this path to the wonderful stay with his new "French brother" and his family? Or was it his original in-class e-mailing to French students that led to his stay in Paris—and a friendship that continues to this day? These two young adults still use technology routinely, from e-mail to Skype to text messaging—in English and French—to keep in touch.

In short, technology helped these two young men—separated by an ocean and six time zones—to connect for the first time and to develop a friendship with another person of another culture who spoke another language, before they even met. Ryan, a teenage student, felt the fear and did it anyway, traveling thousands of miles to meet his new French friend for the first time. The e-mail contact they had had before his arrival allowed him to feel more comfortable with his friend the day he arrived in Paris. He stayed with the boy and his family for two weeks. What did he learn while he was there? He learned not only how to understand and speak French more effectively, but a great deal about the history, art history, geography, and politics of France in conversations with his new second family around their dinner table on the barge and while visiting interesting sites around Paris. What does this teach us? Instead of this being part of a "privileged lifestyle," the trip was a "pay only for the flight" experience that was incredibly rich educationally—and in terms of a new friendship that would last for a lifetime.

It's All about the Kids

If you want to appreciate how e-literate your students are, look through the following list of forms, tools, or "products" that are familiar in what is commonly called new media, social media, and the wide world of electronic communication. How many of these terms do you recognize? How many have you used?

blog, Facebook, Myspace, IM (instant messaging)

You Tube, Listservs, iPhone, iPod, iPad, P2P

e-mail, Wii, podcasting, chat rooms

Twitter, Keek, hyperlink, Wiki

Tumblr, Skype, apps, Oovoo

SMS text, MMS text, FaceTime, Words With Friends

These are terms US youth just hear about and study quickly and efficiently . . . and *get*! This demonstrates just how much technology as a field is growing and how much young people are learning, something that most parents and many teachers know very little or nothing about. Students are making their own way through this electronic milieu very effectively, but wishing for mentors who would allow them to more creatively explore this amazing rain forest, or at least collaborate on planning a great educational journey through it. Children can also be very eager to teach us, their teachers, parents, coaches, and advisers. They are most often patient with our clumsiness as learners, and they are able to add effectively small sprinkles of comic relief. Perhaps this is because they are so familiar with the clumsy experience that learning can be, because they do not fear new bends in the educational road as adults do, and because they have been able to get over more successfully than we have this sometimes frustrating bump in the educational road. I've heard some adept students—starting at middle school age and continuing through high school—say that they wish their teachers knew more about technology. One high school junior said to me, "I guess you have to wait for college for that," referring to learning in a more technologically savvy environment.

Of course, they shouldn't have to "wait for college for that." In many instances, schools have the technology, but lack the vision, direction, or know-how to put the pieces together. Technology is, fortunately, not completely absent in schools, especially because it is so omnipresent in the "world is flat" communities of which it is an important part. But there is a great divide between the "haves" and "have-nots" in terms of technology hardware and software and the knowledge of how to use it. Local businesses, community centers and organizations, and well-off schools could and should provide opportunities for motivated schools or students who are of the "have-nots." A stronger public-private school partnership program we have created at Axis of Hope is one way to achieve this goal in cities and towns across the United States.

I can't, in this book, solve the diverse financial and curricular issues that bedevil so many of our nation's schools. But I can share what I've learned from my students, other young people, and gifted educators and parents whom I have met across the United States and worldwide. Some come from affluent communities and school settings. Others come from distinctly disadvantaged circumstances and backgrounds. But what is clear to so many of them, and so clear to me, is just how universal our children's passion is to learn how to use technology at a profound level. They want to develop native fluency in the latest technology, not only to download and use apps, but to connect with peers beginning in their formative years and beyond, communicating with them in a creative academic—not Facebook social—manner in their schools or homes. Their natural inclination is toward curiosity and rapid acquisition, improvement, and growth in language, in technology, and in every other aspect of development. Given the opportunity—and many youth are searching for those opportunities on the Internet, regardless of school programs—they will work to bridge every kind of divide: both the natural divides of geography, culture, and language, and the manmade, adult-imposed divides of social, political, religious, and educational politics and policy.

We can choose to work with that developmental energy and profound interest, or we can squander it. Of course, there are justifiable concerns. We hear the scary stories of potential exploitation of young people online. The media has reported the pitfalls of the overuse of technology, from cyber-bullying, to online predators, to the rise of ADD and ADHD. What we hear less about, perhaps, is how we, as multitasking parents, use technology as a pacifier for our children; how we, as professionals, attend conferences and often spend our time there buried in our smartphones instead of absorbing any of the often valuable information presented to us; or how we as adults need to be told before driving, watching a movie in a theater, listening to a lecture, or attending a wedding—or a funeral—to turn off our phones. And we complain that our children use technology too much to have fun and are less creative and less active because of it. But how often do we stop and ask if the same is true of us?

The point is, kids aren't waiting for us to connect them with the world. They are doing it themselves. They're making new friends and "colleagues" on the Internet (often, in immature ways, which must be overseen) in online games like Words With Friends; through mobile apps like Draw Something; and on interactive music, art, cinema, and fiction (writing and reading) sites. They're watching foreign language sitcoms and soap operas "together" on websites, and they're playing virtual sports, too, like Madden NFL, Fifa Soccer, and NHL Hockey. Can we drop our defensive, sometimes reflexive negativity toward students' recreational—and educational—use of technology and see it instead as a resource for extraordinary new ways to promote fluency in this area?

Evidence of the new, constructive connections emerging from this twenty-first-century "socializing without borders" is everywhere.

One mother of a high school boy, concerned with how many hours he spent online each week playing one of the popular computer role-playing games (World of Warcraft), watched in curiosity one evening as her son and the other players in the fantasy virtual world outmaneuvered "enemy soldiers." Originally, she had seen his interest as a way to unwind from a demanding workload at school and an after-school job, but she remained a little uneasy about both his commitment to the game (she'd never felt that way about Monopoly, Clue, or any other board game she'd ever played at his age. She was also worried about the potential "creep factor" of it.

Eventually, however, what surprised her was the genuine socializing aspect of the game. Her son would tell her bits and pieces from the online conversation among the participants, who were playing from homes, dorm rooms, and coffee shops with wireless access all over the world. The players kidded around and complained about their teachers or bosses and, in this ongoing weave of one-line quips as they battled ogres, shared their perspectives on the world. He also described to his mother qualities of character that players demonstrated in the way they collaborated on their quests, voted for leadership on various group "raids," discussed disagreements about strategy, and sometimes voted offending players out of a game. It was just a game, a virtual world, but certain aspects of the play—the experience of diverse personalities and communication styles, levels of cooperation, reliability, conflict management, and global conversations—were authentic nonetheless. And, as his mother noticed, in some ways, the quick-reaction skills required to do well at the game mimic those used every day in effective business, governance, and diplomacy.

Recently, another mother shared a similar story with me, surprised by a conversation she had had with her high school freshman son one morning as she drove him to school. Mark had been engrossed in "one of those war games" for some weeks and she was starting to get worried. She had nagged him about it, but his grades were fine, he was active in extracurricular activities at his high school, he spent time with friends (a wholesome enough bunch), and she couldn't find firm ground on which to lecture him. She was peeved anyway, so when he was a little slow getting ready for school one morning, and they'd finally gotten in the car and headed off, she remarked, setting the trap: "So, you've been staying up pretty late because of that computer game lately. Making it hard to get going to school in the morning, is it?" Oblivious to her setup for a sermon, Mark had answered excitedly, tuning in only to the fact that she had noticed he was really into this game and had actually asked him a question instead of registering a complaint. Happy to talk about what he found so exciting, he launched into a description of the game, the challenge, and the strategic choices he was making. The game was one in which the player creates civilizations and manages them through a complex evolution that involves social and political dynamics, economic and industrial development, environmental choices and consequences, leadership and diplomacy. His mother was astonished, first to find herself in an actual conversation with her teenage son instead of giving him a lecture and, second, by what he was saying. As he described what was so cool about the game, she was hearing vocabulary, concepts, critical thinking, problem solving, agility, adaptation, imagination, and moral reasoning that were surprising and reassuring. He'd certainly never talked about his environmental science class that way.

I bring up these out-of-school stories about students using technology to connect with others down the block or around the world in order to collaborate and problem solve, because they hold some wisdom for those of us who want to make the most of technology in schools, classrooms, and at home. First, like the parents who assumed the worst about their children's computer games and were astonished to find just the opposite, we may unconsciously see new technology through old, often clouded lenses—reflexively comparing innovation to tradition or the status quo, dwelling on the difference we define as negative. As educators and parents in that mind-set, if we generally view technology as threatening or lacking substance, we're likely to greet it with trepidation ("I don't know how to do this, and I don't want to look stupid to my students"); suspicion or resentment ("I didn't need computers and the Internet to learn, so neither do my students—or at least not as much as they would like to"); resignation ("I'll use it if I have to, but don't expect me to get excited about it; my lectures will do just fine, thank you"); and resistance ("I'll see that we use it as little as possible"). That's too bad, because if we're worried about losing time learning more about technology or being preoccupied with technology's alleged shortcomings, compared to traditional teaching practices and learning experiences, we not only idealize those often-antiquated, imperfect pedagogical traditions because we're comfortable with them but also are not likely to be open and innovative in researching, learning about, and ultimately using technology to enhance our teaching—and our parenting and our children's learning experiences.

As parents and teachers, we sometimes assume that anything kids do for fun is not really educational, while great theorists such as Piaget and Montessori and decades of research tell us that play is a powerful—perhaps the most powerful—way in which children learn. Their volumes of literature describe play as a catalyst for cognitive and creative development. Play allows children to practice and develop skills, build competencies, and show mastery. If you've ever watched children play computer games, you know how motivated they are to learn the rules, how quickly they pick up the vocabulary and player etiquette, and how eager they are to practice, to acquire, and to perfect their skills.

The Association for the Education of Children International urges educators to incorporate play as a vehicle for learning and all aspects of children's development; on its website, it adds that "many play activities enable children to gain perspectives on the world and to practice culturally sensitive skills that will allow adequate functioning in the global world in which they live. Notable curriculum planning provides for this sensitivity and skill development through play." In generations past, "play" typically meant outdoor play or sports, or indoor play that was hands-on, with art or building materials or socially interactive board games. For this century's children, play also includes technology, whether it is conventional sit-down screen time or more physically interactive activity such as the Wii. We can complain while the world moves ahead, or we can look for ways to capitalize on the connections among kids, technology, and play, and move forward as many other countries already have.

Media Literacy: An Essential for Global Street Smarts

Students need to be able to put technology to work in the service of communication that deepens understanding, strengthens relationships across town and worldwide, and opens new opportunities for them. Here's the kicker: when we use technology to lower cultural walls, we can help youth develop global street smarts they will need in the future, as they begin to learn about and appreciate other societies. Fluency in technology can lead directly to developing fluency in media, too, or what is known as "media literacy." Media literacy, according to the Center for Media Literacy, is "the ability to access, analyze, evaluate, and create media in a variety of forms." Media literacy should play an ever greater role in how students learn to access and interpret information via television, radio, newspapers, magazines, and the Internet. They must be adept at evaluating and synthesizing information, understanding others' ideas, and formulating their own ideas in writing, too.

Using technology as a way to get media into classrooms more quickly and effectively coincides beautifully with a great teacher's desire to meet his or her students where they are already comfortable. We've seen the students who engage in war games, and we know that boys and girls of middle school and high school age have seen plenty of bloody films. Why not meet them where they are, on their turf? If you are studying the Arab-Israeli conflict in a global issues course, for example, you could begin the discussion by showing them the film *To Die in Jerusalem*.

This documentary is about a seventeen-year-old Palestinian girl who becomes a member of a radical pro-Palestinian organization and blows herself up in a Jerusalem supermarket killing a seventeen-year-old Israeli girl as well. The truly scary part of this film is that the girls, whose photos were on the cover of *Time* magazine after this happened, look so much alike that they could be sisters. The Israeli girl had gone grocery shopping to pick something up for her mother (in Israel, suicide bombings have often occurred in public places such as cafés or restaurants where the attacker can affect more people). The Palestinian girl, an elementary school teacher, had recently seen a young student of hers killed by exploding shrapnel from the Israeli army's leveling of a nearby building (the building allegedly housed Hamas members, an extremist Palestinian group classified as a terrorist organization by the Israeli—and US—governments).

The reactions of sixteen- or seventeen-year-old American students after they watch this film in their classrooms are powerful. What if you then connect these students via live videoconference (or Skype) with teenage Palestinian and Israeli students living in the Middle East? You'll hear the Palestinian or Israeli students say, "Oh yeah, we knew about that when it happened [in 2002]. We were younger then, but we knew about it." Thanks to technology, this connection makes the events portrayed in the film even more real and animates the students in this country further as they discuss the history of the Arab-Israeli conflict, the division of Jerusalem, the first and second intifada—and the possibility of a third intifada as well.

Once the students are engaged on this level, you can make the move to improved media literacy. Have students go back to that tragedy and see how it was reported in the newspapers. How was it depicted by the *Jerusalem Post*, Al Jazeera (the Arabic language news network, translated into English), the BBC, CNN, Fox News, the *New York Times*, or local newspapers or television stations. Ask students to investigate where the story was placed: was it in the upper right corner of the front page, or in the upper left corner? Was it on page three or four, in the lower left corner? How big was the font? Students will start to understand and become savvy media users and consumers. Any time you are studying a geopolitical conflict in the world—teaching students about Kashmir, for example—any time a story is being covered by global media sources, you might have students find at least six sources online that present the same story in different ways. This is an excellent introduction to how the media can and will manipulate stories. Technology can make all of this available quickly and with the most basic of setups (a laptop connected to an LCD projector, for example).

After students have begun to develop improved media literacy, you can present a modern-day situation, perhaps something happening in Jerusalem today. By showing the way this news story is reported, but obscuring its source, you can then ask students who is depicting the story. And students will start to understand the importance of looking from many different angles at a conflict or any issue in the media as one might look at a work of art. The great challenge of global understanding can be enhanced immeasurably by media literacy that demonstrates multiple points of view and the reasons for each perspective. And a final important thought: the ability to formulate arguments with evidence from primary and secondary sources such as these plays directly into new state common core standards.

What We Can Do Now

- Use technology to enhance foreign language pedagogy in myriad ways: purchase and download programs such as Rosetta Stone for your foreign language students, for example, or purchase language textbook software, often valuable in planning and executing good lesson plans.
- Attend foreign language teacher association workshops and conferences (ACTFL, MaFLA, and so on) to learn from other great language teachers how to enhance foreign language courses with technology.
- Gear online or other recreational computer use toward learning objectives first, then encourage global networking and other creative applications of existing activities to reach these objectives. Examples: virtual visits of Paris and Skype calls with students living there to improve student understanding and use of spoken French.

- If you're inexperienced or uncomfortable with technology, go immediately to your school's director of technology or IT department. One person or a team of people can be amazingly helpful in answering your questions about using technology to enhance your courses. If your school does not have a director of technology or other IT resource and you need help immediately, ask your students. They will be only too glad to demonstrate their skills and be teachers to you.
- Sponsor a technology fair once a year at your school. Hold a student competition for interesting and innovative technology projects, similar to the science project fair hosted by the White House each year. This tradition will allow the winners to display their impressive work for other members of the school community. These could include the best PowerPoint presentations, the best e-mail or Skype chats, or the best short foreign language films or commercials, or new grammar software, all of which build language skills while reinforcing and sharing cultural awareness in a potpourri of creative narratives. You can also tap parents of varied cultures to provide delicious food and drink at these fairs.
- Conduct a laptop video conference with an expert in your subject area. Such exposure, perhaps to a level just above the students' current level (i.e., high school students conversing with a college professor or middle school students conversing with a standout high school teacher), can and will bring lecture material alive—you can tell by the quality of questions that your students will ask.
- Experiment with creating all of your teaching lessons in PowerPoint as a different perspective for engaging your students' interest. Make a webpage for your class, with course syllabi, assignments, practice tests, and quizzes included. Also, have students respond to some assignments online, where they can read each other's responses and comment on them any day at any time.

- In foreign language courses, have students in each language level create PowerPoint presentations in the target language that they can then show to classmates. Students in beginner French courses, for example, can be assigned to create PowerPoint presentations on French-speaking cities (for example, Paris, Montreal, Dakar), regions (Normandy, Brittany, Provence, Quebec), or small countries (Martinique and so on). In intermediate French classes, students can be assigned to create presentations dealing with important people in French history (Napoleon, Louis Pasteur, Marie Curie, and so on). In advanced intermediate French courses, they could create presentations dealing with important French writers or poets they are studying (Victor Hugo, Baudelaire, Camus, and more).
- Have students use computers to create spreadsheets of verb conjugations or chapter study guides for themselves and others in the class before test time.
- Use computers to play popular music by Spanish, French, Mandarin, or Arabic rock groups not just to liven up class time, but to help students train their ears to the spoken language, to learn vocabulary and idioms, and to feel connected to the teen culture of another country.

CHAPTER FOUR

Travel Opportunities and the Fluency of Extracurricular Activities

Improving our children's global IQ can begin in their earliest years and in the simplest ways, and the options for doing so begin wherever we take the initiative to envision them. Inspiration is all around us, not only from current local, national, and global events but from historic times as well. I like to think of Christopher Columbus in this context. Columbus isn't the all-star icon he once was in American myth, having shifted over time from celebrated explorer to early exploiter of indigenous peoples, but at least one part of his mythic story holds a fresh thought for us today. Columbus grew up in Genoa, a bustling port town in northern Italy. His global IQ was already well developed as a result of his surroundings. In this vibrant center of fifteenth-century culture and commerce, the fourteen-year-old son of a wool merchant took a liking to those from other cultures who moored in Genoa's port. He was attracted to the sea as well, and the rest, as they say, is history. The stimulating, cosmopolitan culture in which he spent those early years is an image worth keeping in mind as we look for ways to create schools, homes, and communities like that bustling fifteenth-century town that cultivate children's curiosity and confidence in exploring the world.

Such exploration in this educational context, as we will discover in this chapter, can begin close to home. It can take place in our homes; we can watch foreign films, prepare dishes reflecting other cultures, or even host a foreign exchange student. Or it can extend to the farthest corners of the globe in such popular service-learning locations as South Africa and India. Improving our children's global IQ takes all these opportunities, deploying them in different, creative ways, given the age group, course of study, budgetary allowance, learning goals, and more. Take Steven Berbeco's Arabic language program at Boston's Charlestown High School. In April 2011, Steven arranged a trip for some of his students from both his academic year and summer high school programs to travel to Qatar, a small, oil-rich Arab country in the Middle East. The ten-day trip was a once-in-a-lifetime introduction to life in Qatar for Boston-area high school students studying Arabic. There, the US students studied and lived alongside Qatari high school students, visited interesting cultural sites, tasted new foods, and practiced their Arabic. And the best part? It was entirely funded by Qatar Foundation International, a non-profit organization run by the government of Qatar. Everything was paid for, from the moment the students departed from Boston's Logan Airport to their return to their supportive families ten days later. The foundation was so sensitive to the needs of the American students that any individual who needed extra financial assistance purchasing luggage or appropriate clothing received that stipend immediately and without question.

Clearly, Steven had been doing his homework and used his passion and networking skills to make this opportunity for his students a reality. But, in his pedagogy, Steven also includes multiple other opportunities for traveling right here at home. His summer program, for example, takes an annual field trip to Boston's Greenway open market. There, among numerous other delicacies, there is an Arabic-speaking olive and date vendor, a nut vendor, and a pita and bagel vendor—all a mere three miles from Charlestown High School. And do you remember how I welcomed Proctor Academy students to their study abroad trimester in France? After lessons in bargaining in Arabic, Steven's students split into small groups for their field trip. Each is charged with procuring something different for the delectable open-air picnic the entire class will share later that day. And there, with foods that reflect Arabic-speaking cultures, the students are able to practice their Arabic language skills. How does this creative example of Steven's Arabic pedagogy apply to what other teachers can do to improve their school's global IQ? What can we do to make each classroom—and each living room and dining room—a small, bustling port town of ideas from around the world, rather than a cocoon snuffing our youths' inquisitive flames? We can take the time to research sites in local areas that reflect the shrinking planet and then take our students or sons and daughters there with us. In the Boston area alone, examples of local sites include Chinatown, the North End and its Italian influence, and the Museum of Fine Arts, to name but a few.

To have more ships of ideas docking in our homes and schools, we do not need to send all our youth overseas, although study abroad before graduating from high school in the United States is undoubtedly a great way to jumpstart study of a new language or to introduce students to other cultures. However, many school districts do not have the necessary budgets to send students to France, China, Latin America, or Qatar. We must instead think creatively, bringing assembly or school meeting speakers representing global cultures, ideas, and activities into our schools to share their valuable international perspectives. We must harness available technology to bring international figures or peers from other countries virtually face-to-face with our students, as discussed in the previous chapter. We can provide educational vessels that our students can board—assigning them creative projects, like inventing new foreign language online games or writing short stories in another language to make available online—to take risks as Columbus did, circumnavigating our new world in more creative ways.

The Corkscrew Effect

The corkscrew is a familiar tool: a single metal helix attached to a handle. Just as the multiple rungs help the corkscrew grip the inside of the cork and provide additional surface area and torque for the job of pulling the cork out of a bottle, so revisiting the issue of globalization multiple times in a child's course of study in middle school or high school, during her or his formative years, provides the enhanced familiarity critical to giving the mind a firm grip on this concept. In many important respects, the road to globalization of education has been paved by the wonderful work of international program directors who have recently overseen initiatives in countless US public, private, and parochial schools. In addition to maps of the United States in K–12 classrooms, maps of other continents and of the entire world have been added. An example of this: I have used a map of the world with younger students several times. First, I give each student two pins and a long piece of colored string or yarn. I say, "Go home and ask Mom and Dad about the heritage of your family. If Mom and Dad have families that originally came from more than one foreign country, even multiple countries, we'll give you more pins." The idea is to put one pin in the map where the child is currently living and the next pin or pins where her or his ancestors came from. The piece of yarn is then stretched between the two pins in a colorful and dramatic rendering of diversity and our shrinking, interconnected planet.

The question "Where in the world did your relatives come from?" starts a lot of conversations, too. A particular student's roots may lie in Portugal, for example, or another may have a mother whose family is from China, while the father's is originally from Germany. Because there are different colored pieces of yarn, and the students ask questions and gain a more profound perspective about the heritage of their own and other students' families, the students often then feel more comfortable disclosing that they speak Portuguese or another language at home or that they are trilingual, speaking English at school and German and Mandarin at home. You can then take the class out to a Portuguese, Chinese, or German restaurant, or even better, ask one of the parents to bring in clothing from her or his native land, with different native dishes for the students to taste.

Such interaction, in the already familiar setting of the students' classroom, is incredibly powerful for two reasons. The first is the experiential quality of not just teaching one skill but appealing to all five senses: hearing another language, tasting and smelling another cuisine, feeling the texture of the clothing. Imagine the mother of one of the students, from another culture and society, entering the classroom with clothing covering her entire body except for her eyes. She offers students a dish of olives, cucumbers, and humus with lemon and a smoky eggplant dip with torn pieces of flatbread. Being able to globalize all five of the students' senses like this in their formative years is key to breaking down the barriers that many students have from speaking only English and knowing exactly what they will order each time at the McDonald's drive-through.

The second reason that this creative interaction has such an impact is because the appeal to students' senses is done in a familiar setting, their own classroom, where they are comfortable and where their minds—and eyes, ears, noses, and taste buds—are open to receiving, processing, digesting, and retaining all these new ideas. In a corkscrew effect, as the brain develops and as we continue to work the idea of globalization into students' brains, we find more opportunities to engage in activities not only inside the school, but outside. Maybe the age group or the budget doesn't warrant a trip to France for middle school students studying the French language, but how about a trip to an art museum to see and learn about Impressionist paintings? Or what about a trip to a university to hear a tenured French professor speak about author and pilot Saint-Exupéry and his classic book *The Little Prince*? Or a weekend trip to Quebec or to northern Vermont where a large French-speaking population has migrated from Canada? Or to New Orleans, where French Creole is spoken, and spicy Cajun food is served around the city each day?

For Spanish, before going to Latin America to advance immersion in the Spanish language, how about taking students to a Mexican restaurant or a Spanish restaurant specializing in tapas? Or having students host a bake sale and a car wash to raise money for a trip to Little Havana in Miami, or areas closer to home where Latino peoples and cultures have settled? Such travel can be completed by bus, the number of nights required for lodging reduced as a result. Schools in the area being visited often offer gyms as places to sleep and hot showers to use, as well. The linguistic and cultural experience, the saturation that has such a profound effect on students, can be retained while fueling Christopher Columbus type journeys right from the very beginning.

I am not trying to rehabilitate Columbus's character for the history books, but I believe we can make fresh use of his story in redefining the meaning of expansionism. (Howard Zinn, a friend and colleague at Boston University until his death, had quite a bit to say about the exploitation of people in the Americas.) In Columbus's day, and through more than two hundred years of US history, the goal of expansionism was for increased economic exploitation and geographic and religious growth. In the twenty-first century, the new US practice of expansionism could—and should—represent our tireless efforts to expand our students' understanding of, communication with, and positive interactions with other countries and cultures, beginning with what we teach in their classrooms each day.

Travel and Study Abroad

For a student living and growing up in the United States, the limited scope of "What did you get on the test?" and "Who won the game?" in our schools, added to the distorting lens of a fast-food, throwaway, air-conditioned mall culture outside of classrooms and sports fields, is difficult to overcome. It can lead to a hardening of students' linguistic and cultural arteries, which can keep them from effectively improving global literacy. But short trips give a glimpse of the world beyond the familiar linguistic and cultural field of vision. Such vision can be expanded further when a family decides to host an exchange student from another country, as one of my brothers and his family did. Imagine the discussions around the dining room table. Then, encouraging our students to live in another culture for a long period of time, immersed in a different language and culture, removes the lens entirely.

A student begins with a comfort zone of familiarity, but eventually must make that choice to "feel the fear and do it anyway"—to take a courageous step forward, to depart rather than remain in the calm home port, in the classroom, in the school halls, or around the dining room table. How does a young person find the confidence to take that risk and venture outside of her or his linguistic and cultural comfort zone? I think it is most often through the combined influence of parents, teachers, peers, and siblings, or inspiring talks they hear, or perhaps in listening to others share personal stories of their own experiences in casual conversations.

My hope is that more middle and upper school students who are able to take advantage of such opportunities seriously consider a short or more extended period of study abroad, before they go to college. Beginning with the first steps we can help our own children take early in life, we can help students to help themselves improve global IQ. The bridges we can build to encourage and cultivate global competency and sensibilities in our children—from the corkscrew activities through one- to two-week foreign language trips and sports trips (discussed later in the chapter)—teachers can support students' study abroad for one week, one summer, one semester, a full year, and/or even a gap year after high school.

A former student of mine, Frank, a top student-athlete (a star tennis player), told me that his study abroad and immersion into Spain's culture during a gap year before attending Harvard led him to view the world's countless cultures in a different way:

> Until I lived away from our American culture that I had always accepted as the best, or if not the best, then the one that was the most powerful, and therefore the best to follow . . . I had never been exposed to a different culture. Before traveling I never questioned our own culture, but now I see things in American culture (and Spanish culture) that I don't necessarily buy into. I find myself questioning the way we eat, the way we drink, the way we work, the way we deal with conflict. I can't say whose culture is better—"ours or theirs"—but now that I've lived in a different culture I am more aware of and open to different ways of life.

This perspective reveals improved global IQ, the goal of what we can hope to provide for more youth. Students who travel to another country, especially if they stay for an extended period to live and study or work, as Frank did, find it to be an eye-opening, mind-opening, intellectual, and sensory experience that is transformative. The first goals of travel and study abroad are cultural and linguistic immersion: making the constant effort to live the language and culture, preferably with a host family. (In a dorm setting with other Americans, some students may retreat from the challenge of engagement and will often fall back on the comfort of English when speaking with friends.) Those who want to get the most out of their foreign stay always find a way to take themselves out of the cultural and linguistic cocoon and into the local milieu. Whether it is over conversations in cafés, playing on a local youth soccer team (or the Institute of Political Science rugby team, as I did during my junior year abroad in college in the early 1980s), or living with a marvelous host family, as I did in Paris at that same time, there are many ways to join in local activities with peers, new friends, and new hosts.

Typically, when students return from a year of study abroad, or even a semester or a few weeks traveling or studying overseas, we see phenomenal growth in their level of maturity, their global competency, and even their thinking regarding the future of their education and careers, compared to their peers at home. Students tell me that their experience of acculturation and interdependence while living abroad, typically quite challenging, enables them to

- Figure out how to live in other cultures and traditions as chameleons who learn not only to fit in, but to respect those languages, cultures, and traditions as well.
- Learn other languages more swiftly and effectively (and when learning another language, they discover which verbs to learn first: to be, to have, to do, to come, to go, to eat, to drink).
- Study hard, exercising the mind every day while being immersed in another language and culture, whether focused on study or casual pursuits such as conversations in a café or watching television in the target language, building stronger intellectual "muscles" in terms of linguistic and cultural understanding and expression.
- Become more open not only to other people's languages and cultures but also to their ideas and suggestions, and their often varied points of view.
- Begin to more fully appreciate—or to criticize with maturity—certain aspects of life or thinking in the United States that

previously they took for granted or did not question, such as monolingualism, monoculturalism, and the "we are the greatest nation on earth" mentality of many.

- Begin to see ways in which the United States could be more responsible as a globally minded, friendly neighbor and more welcome as a partner in the global community.
- Feel their power as individuals to contribute as global citizens and to be agents for change and growth in their *own* schools and communities.

Travel and study abroad teaches students about other cultures and languages, giving them a more profound awareness of other communities, which they can apply when they return home. When they are in other countries, they realize that what they do affects others in an interconnected web. At the same time, it teaches them about themselves, their own potential, and the roles they can play as active participants in whatever arena they choose in our increasingly interdependent world. The ripple makes its way out to the widest concentric circle, the student's family, school community, and beyond, and returns all the way back to the initial source, the student herself or himself.

Cross-curricular, Extracurricular Interests as Bridges to Travel

The above examples seem to indicate that school-sponsored trips abroad are almost exclusively the province of foreign language students. That used to be the case. For years, beginning in the 1960s, French, Spanish, German, and Russian were the extent of the language courses offered in many US middle and high schools. The vast majority of overseas trips for students and teachers offered at most public, private, and parochial schools in the United States, if they sponsored any trips, focused on countries where these languages—or English—were spoken. There is no longer any logical reason that it has to remain that way. Maybe it is still that way in your school.

But it is time to rethink overseas travel. Foreign travel has now become a window into the improving pedagogy in the fields of Chinese and Arabic in US schools, as well as in the fields of history, art, music, theater, debate, science, even sports; any aspect of academic or student life can provide the basis for exciting travel and study opportunities inside or outside the United States. If the fluency being shared is not a language but an activity, such as soccer or singing, the connections can be even more immediate and more profound. Let me share one wonderful example.

In June 1995, I took a middle school boys' baseball team—twelve seventh and eighth graders from the Boston area—to Puerto Rico for a cultural and athletic experience I'd been able to arrange through 1st Sports Tours, Inc., a tour company that specializes in school sports-related trips to different parts of the world for youth and adults. The company was assisted in the planning of this trip by the joint collaboration of the Roberto Clemente Foundation (supporters of youth baseball in Puerto Rico), the Puerto Rico Tourist Company, and the Puerto Rico Commissioner of Baseball. The program was designed to combine baseball, recreation—especially on the beach in San Juan—sightseeing, and community service, just after our spring baseball season and academic year had ended in mid-June.

The sports program included several friendly baseball games with two local Puerto Rican teams of seventh- and eighth-grade boys. Small groups of the host teams' parents and siblings attended the games, and were a source of great excitement, cheering, and laughter. And baseball is a passion in Puerto Rico, so not coincidentally the local youth teams' skills were very impressive. All the boys—the Puerto Rican and the American boys alike—played to win, but they also played with great sportsmanship, camaraderie, and class. At one scheduled game, the host team was short a few players, so both teams came together as one large group and then divided up to make two new teams combining players from each original team. Despite the language barrier (many of the boys were not from my Spanish class), the boys shared the universal language of baseball, about which all were excited and in which all were clearly well versed.

One of the most enlightening lessons of the trip, as the boys recalled, came after we first arrived at the Roberto Clemente Foundation baseball field, where we would be playing for the first time, fresh off our flight from Boston, with a stopover in Miami and then the thirty-minute bus ride from the San Juan International Airport. As we schlepped all our equipment under a blazing sun, across the outfield of carefully groomed grass and a stunning, ochre-colored clay infield, unsure which dugout was ours, the boys noticed something that caught their attention. Behind both benches were large, shoebox-shaped green nets—each about twenty-feet long and twelve-feet high—similar to, but somewhat smaller than, the batting cages you see behind many Little League and Babe Ruth League baseball fields in the States. Each net was partitioned on the inside to provide two smaller practice spaces. The boys could see from a distance that inside each half of the batting cages, there was one teenage boy and one younger boy or girl, maybe five or six years old, facing one another from opposite ends of the cages. My players had never seen a practice drill like this before and couldn't figure it out, so they walked over to one cage for a closer look.

Inside the cage, a boy of about fifteen was on his knees facing a younger boy, who was also on his knees, about five yards away. Neither had a baseball glove. The older boy would roll a baseball slowly on the ground to the younger boy, who would have to pick up the ball, bring it up in a smooth arc from the ground to his chest and then to his right ear, and throw the ball back very slowly and precisely, aiming for the older boy's chest. The younger boy was learning to field ground balls and throw them back to the correct spot, on his knees. When one of the US boys asked the older boy why he was doing this on his knees, the boy explained (in Spanish, which I translated) that there were several reasons. The "on the knees" position kept the younger players from overexerting their arms in practice; also, they learned balance on their knees before they developed balance on their feet. And the older boy knew that by lowering himself to the younger child's level for the early portion of the practice, he had "leveled the playing field" with his body language, acting as a mentor while remaining on a par with the younger child.

After some time rolling the ground balls, the older boy started to throw slightly higher, little "looper" fly balls, and the younger boy, still on his knees, would focus on the flies, catch them, and throw them back to the older boy, as he had the grounders. After a time, the little boy got to use a bat, too, but still while on his knees. As the older boy would throw the ball softly to the younger boy, he would hit that ball back to the older boy, aiming not for the chest area but to spots just to the right or just to the left of the older boy, like carefully placing his hits to produce base hits. Eventually, the young boy was batting from a full standing position, and the older boy used white athletic tape to mark spots on the inside of the netting as targets for the hitter. He moved the target spot from time to time, so the young batter would have to adjust his position to hit the new spot.

Watching the young Puerto Rican boys and their young coaches, we were able to see clearly that they both appeared to enjoy this practice style, and we realized that this was a very important mentoring tradition in the Puerto Rican baseball culture. The fifteen-year-old boys had learned this way themselves as five and six year olds, and now they were acting as the teachers, coaches, and mentors, giving back in their own way to the young children coming up through the baseball ranks. It was also fascinating for us to observe the older, adult coaches, as they strolled back and forth between the practice cages, making suggestions to the younger coaches every so often, all in a relaxed, respectful team manner. We could see how much fun it was for all the boys—and some young girls as well—and just how this physical training style was so fluid and respectful of the body and developing musculature of the younger players. Both groups of boys and girls were learning. The older boys were learning how to be good coaches and improve their own techniques in the process of teaching. And the younger children were obviously delighted to have the attention and guidance from the "cool" older boys. My own students, though closer in age to the older boys, instantly related to the delight of the little ones in having been taken under the wing of these supportive, older boys. It was an eye-opening experience in how well baseball is taught in Puerto Rico, one that impressed me and my students. They were eager to talk about it and brainstorm about possible variations that might work in their own communities upon their return home.

In addition to witnessing this creative Puerto Rican form of a Big Brother/Big Sister mentoring program in youth baseball, our service-learning portion of the trip took us to the San Juan Health Center, where one morning my student-athletes volunteered to work with physically and intellectually disabled children (more about US service-learning activities can be found in chapter 8). My students helped in a variety of ways, combining recreation and physical therapy using ball games. They approached their activities in inventive ways. As the boys used inflatable beach balls to throw or roll to the disabled patients, they were asking themselves, "How might we apply the skills we witnessed in those small baseball cages to assisting these special needs children?" The challenge: the handicaps these young people faced, and figuring out how to create a confidence-building experience of fun and success for them, no matter what their circumstance. I was impressed by how quickly and seamlessly my student-athletes were able to invent new and gentle activities that the children and adults absolutely loved. One seventh grader from Wayland, Massachusetts, set up ten capped felt-tip pens, which he called bowling pins, on the floor near a wall. Then he taught the handicapped children, many of whom were in wheelchairs, to bowl a beach ball and try to knock down the pins. The game was a hit.

Our trip, which also included such in-hotel pranks as coating hotel-room door handles with shaving cream and placing small, plastic wastebaskets full of water on top of barely opened doors, proved to be an extraordinary linguistic, cultural, and athletic learning experience for my students. It was also an incredible bonding experience, adding a new dimension to our student-teacher, coach, adviser relationship that helped me to coach better and helped the boys to play even better as a team. The boys were thrilled to engage with others who shared their sports interest and the language of baseball, even without a common native language.

There are many more ways in which a child's global IQ can be enhanced through extracurricular activities, such as playing baseball in Puerto Rico. As you develop your own new ideas, remember that we are not seeking to reinvent the wheel, only to take what we are already doing and apply it in the service of globalization. Remember, this is a renaissance, not a renovation.

Democratizing the Global Travel and Study Experience

It would be too simplistic for me to say, "Where there's a will, there's a way." At the same time, I do believe that social, political, and economic possibilities follow genuine interest and a profound desire for change much more easily than they follow disinterest or apathy. So it follows that there is another question—"Do we truly want to make it possible for our students to travel and study abroad before they graduate from high school?"—that comes before "How do we pay for all of this?"

There are many variations of this one basic question, which reflects a host of objections, from practical considerations to reflexive reactions. For example: If students wish to go overseas, will you lose key members of the community (students, teachers, administrators) for part or all of the year? How will these people be replaced effectively, in the classroom and during sports seasons, by exchange teachers and students or by local part-time substitute employees? Will grades from the programs be transferable to the home educational institution? Should they be? Will US students be able to take standardized exams such as the MCAS, SAT, SAT II, and AP when they are studying abroad? How are these programs vetted? How are students or teachers monitored when they are overseas? What rules and regulations should be employed (i.e., regarding alcohol, smoking, curfews)? And the list goes on and on.

Once these questions are answered—or considered, depending on their relative merit—a different set of questions about expenses and logistics emerges: Is there a possibility of establishing exchanges between your school and schools in different parts of the world reflecting the foreign language courses offered at your school? Are parents willing to support and provide some of the investment, perhaps in lieu of another purchase they were planning to make for the school, themselves, or their families? Can the school seek all or partial funding from grants, or the support of donors, or local businesses? Can you hold a bake sale, a car wash, or a silent auction to help defray the expenses?

Opportunities for global interaction, for travel and study abroad, are already available to a wide range of students, especially in affluent independent schools and public schools in upscale parts of the country, and provided that communities are committed to how much they will benefit from these opportunities. Many of the programs do offer scholarships, which is an excellent first step in assisting the have-nots more effectively. But we need to do a better job of encouraging students from diverse communities to find the programs that provide financial aid and to apply for them. Perhaps most importantly, we have to give them the cultural capital to even know that these programs exist. One excellent example is Boston-based Quest Adventures. According to president and founder Claudia Bell, Quest Adventures "supports teams of Boston public high school students and teachers to reach out to others, both in the US and abroad, in the spirit of community service."

In my travels and in interactions with students visiting the United States from other countries or traveling within their own countries, I have met remarkable young people from across the economic spectrum. Some have been the children of leaders or wealthy members of their communities; others have come from more modest circumstances, and some, as with the students from the Rwandan school for orphans we will meet in the next part of this book, have come from homes with extremely limited financial resources. Whatever some may lack in financial wealth, and even in formal education, they are not at all lacking in their capacity to wholeheartedly pursue myriad chances for "international travel," even if that means to another part of their own town, city, state, or country, and to learn and grow profoundly from it. Every student with the curiosity and courage to travel "abroad" has the prerequisites for a stimulating, successful learning experience and the capacity to enrich his or her community in new ways upon return.

There are young people from every neighborhood, town, and city in the United States who want to study abroad, who want to learn, grow, and become active and engaged participants in the world they will enter as adults. We need to do everything in our power to make it possible for them to become global citizens and to improve their global IQs, rather than allowing our fears and concerns—real or imagined—to become obstacles.

"The Thirteenth Year": The Wisdom of a Gap Year

In my years of travel, scores of traveling students I have crossed paths with are eighteen- and nineteen-year-old recent high school graduates, from New Zealand, Australia, and Great Britain especially, who are living on a shoestring while traveling around the world for six months to a year before they enter college. They share stories about doing volunteer work in orphanages in Latin America, or in elementary schools for disadvantaged youth in Thailand, or in soup kitchens in New Delhi or Johannesburg. The more stories I hear, the more I realize that this is rarely the case in the United States, because college counselors, most high school administrators, college undergraduate admissions officers, and parents support the immediate move from high school to undergraduate study in colleges, rather than a year off—or a gap year—after high school.

Why don't more US students take a gap year? And why do so many teachers and administrators, the schools' college counselors, and the students' parents—and peers—encourage the students to remain on what I call "the academic gerbil wheel"? They are running or sprinting with no end in sight to do well in high-pressure high school academic courses, do well on standardized exams, get glowing letters of recommendation, and go to a wonderful college with a big name, only to think after arriving about which graduate school they would like to attend. Part of the reason is that high schools, especially well-to-do suburban public and independent high schools, brag about and/or use the colleges their graduates attend in their marketing to prospective students and parents. Numerous teachers also feel quite understandably that how their students score on standardized exams is the grading system used for them as teachers. But why must we brag about where our students—especially those for whom we write college letters of recommendation—go to college? Parents, too, often love to speak about where their children are going to attend college, at cocktail parties, sports matches, and elsewhere. On the surface, there is nothing wrong with this pride in where our children are going to college. The issues arise when our unquestioned drive makes us hesitate to allow students to study overseas during their middle and high school years or to experience a year off after high school to deepen their reservoir of personal experiences and self-knowledge before attending college.

Perhaps parental reluctance to have a child travel far from home for a whole or part of a year is related to the post-9/11 fears of many in the United States and to the unstable geopolitical climate in certain areas such as Egypt, Syria, Lebanon, Israel, Haiti, Kenya, and other countries currently on the US State Department's travel warnings list. Perhaps this reluctance is due, as some parents have told me, to the financial consequences of delaying college by a year and facing the inevitably higher tuition costs the following year, and for three years after that. Whatever the reason for the reluctance or inertia, I'd like to offer several good reasons to encourage more US high school graduates to take a year to grow before they go to college.

Many, perhaps most, high school students feel caught in a market-driven educational world where grades and diplomas are often all that really count. The idea of informal, experiential education as something worthwhile that enriches the life of the mind is almost quaint in our competitive education and career marketplace. But increasingly in today's world—and in tomorrow's world—when global experience speaks, people listen. I have never heard a college admissions officer suggest that a student is a less attractive applicant after spending a summer, semester, or year engaged in meaningful work or travel to broaden his or her life experience. I have heard the opposite: that a student who has taken a calculated risk and done something interesting with a gap year—especially global travel, study, and/or service learning, all blending together to create a transformative experience—has more to offer a college as an applicant.

As an educator, a father, and a consultant to schools across the United States and around the world, I believe that youth should get out and explore during their teenage years. They should pay attention to what draws them in, excites them, and intrigues them, and what they are passionate about. Time off will not only recharge their physical and emotional batteries but will expose students to new places and people and ideas that could become their passions, as well. These intuitive choices most often lead to the most successful, creative, multifaceted ventures in college, career, and life. High school students need to hear that it is often a good idea—not a sign of a slacker—to take a break from academia and recharge their batteries, especially after an incredibly rigorous, competitive high school experience. Adolescents should be allowed to get off the academic treadmill for a short while to recover from burnout and to gain exposure to new languages, cultures, and experiences, immersed in others' lands, ideas, and homes, half a state or half a world away. As Fred Hargadon, former dean of admissions at Princeton University, has stated: "The ideal age to enter the freshman class is twenty-one, not eighteen."

I would argue that a high school graduate will be better able to pick a college and a possible major after a gap-year experience; also, she or he arrives at a college during her or his freshman year with a fresh, more open mind, very often with more focus and intention about getting the most from the college experience. As reported by Andrew Jones, a British government-funded research program found that students who took a gap year not only spent more years in college but were also more focused on what they wanted to do there. Jones found that at age nineteen, not at eighteen, and after a year of calculated risk taking, students were more confident about their academic and career directions.

Gap-year students often see a different way of living and are able to redefine their goals in life based on their newfound interests, and where they have been and will want to go in the world, too. Whatever they do will be more on their own terms, because they have had a new, hands-on experience of independent living. One student I interviewed never wanted to be a teacher until she had taught in an elementary school in Rwanda during her gap year. As a result, she rewrote her college applications in order to attend a teacher's college the following year. This is one example of the impact a gap year can have on a student's global IQ; it can be transformative.

What We Can Do Now

- Explore short-term travel possibilities at your school, during the academic year vacations, overseas or in the United States. Find out if these programs can be expanded to areas of focus beyond just tourist interests (such as cultural exchange trips for sports, like the Puerto Rico trip, or the arts, like a trip for a school choir to give performances while traveling).
- Prepare carefully an excellent, understandable predeparture package for students and their parents, otherwise known as a "predeparture program orientation materials." (See the resources at the end of the book.) Involve other teachers, administrators, students, and families in the preparation; for example, ask a colleague to speak to students about the history of the place they will visit.
- Keep in constant contact with students and program leaders while they are overseas (weekly phone conversations with US program directors, or weekly phone or e-mail contact with students and faculty overseas). Use technology for live feeds from overseas, like Skype, if possible. Try to teach students and their parents *not* to remain in constant contact while the students are traveling abroad, though. This is an important part of teaching students to be more mature and gradually appeasing parental fear, lessons that you are trying to teach students and their parents in order to improve their global IQ.
- When students return to school after their travel or study abroad, follow up with them in a debriefing focused on the

quality of the off-campus program and overall experience. Have students put together a presentation about their trip and offer it to part or all of the school community, to foreign language classes, at a faculty meeting, or at a board of trustees or school board meeting.

- Encourage other ways for students to share their travel experiences, such as creating a photo display in the halls of the school, writing an article for the school or local paper, or blogging for the school website.

PART TWO

ACTION STEPS

CHAPTER FIVE

Preventive Diplomacy

In this part of the book, I want to share the idea of preventive diplomacy as a compelling educational model for engaging students in the hands-on work of communication, compromise, creativity, collaboration, and consensus building with other young people, as well as experts, working to prevent conflict in the world more effectively. It is what I call "a revolution of conflict resolution." Exhilarating, pioneering work is underway in this field. Our children don't have to wait to get out in the real world to start learning about and practicing conflict management and prevention. In this chapter, I will outline the principles and practices of preventive diplomacy, and then in chapters 6 and 7, I will show preventive diplomacy at work, using what I call the "intellectual Outward Bound" case study approach with students.

Why do I devote so much attention to this material? Because in a broad sense, a preventive diplomacy curriculum might be the single-best introduction to global IQ, conveyed through all the components discussed to this point. Preventive diplomacy utilizes progressive foreign language opportunities and instruction; an integrated, innovative use of technology; media literacy that enables students to effectively evaluate the quality of information they find or receive about the areas of the United States—and the world—they are studying; and the experiential learning that comes from conducting live, hands-on conflict-resolution negotiations, without leaving the classroom. Important local, national, and global issues facing us today need to be studied and then enacted (rather than simply read about) to truly come alive. Through the preventive diplomacy case-study approach, role-playing exercises in geopolitical conflict resolution include training students about the history of particular cultures (religious, political, geographic, and socioeconomic issues such as the Arab-Israeli conflict) as well as about the important peoples involved in these intergroup conflicts. The students work in their classrooms with extensive supplementary materials and resources, relying on insights that now define successful approaches used in business and government.

Preventive diplomacy has had a long and somewhat loosely defined, yet instrumental role in international relations. Notable world leaders and foreign policy experts have recognized it as one of the most powerful alternatives to armed conflict and essential if we are to prevent globally catastrophic wars and violence. Former UN Secretary-General Boutros Boutros-Ghali described preventive diplomacy as "diplomatic action to prevent existing disputes from arising between parties, to prevent these disputes from escalating into conflicts and to limit the spread of the latter when they occurred." This nonmilitary strategy has indeed been helpful to some extent in quelling armed conflict between nations or peoples in chronic conflict, addressing areas of potential crisis before they erupt in repeated violence in such places as Bosnia, the Kashmir region, and North and South Korea.

Another respected advocate of preventive diplomacy, Mohammed Bedjaoui, a judge on the International Court of Justice (the World Court) at The Hague, writes that in today's small, interconnected world, a "fundamental truth must be tirelessly reiterated: What affects one country affects the others. And the nascent truth of today will be an absolute truth as mutual dependency becomes reinforced." Bedjaoui echoes the thoughts of many of us in the field when he describes contemporary preventive diplomacy as a vibrant arena and urges that "preventive diplomacy must broaden its horizon in order to build on the planetary scale."

Yet, I present a somewhat different view of preventive diplomacy to students, teachers, administrators, and parents. It is in many ways a corollary to Boutros Boutros-Ghali's definition. To prevent future conflicts more effectively, *students* must be taught when they are young sponges to be more globally intelligent. They must be prepared to understand more thoroughly the constantly evolving ethical, legal, religious, social, environmental, and political implications of local, national, and global conflict, and the often-complex roots of these conflicts. We must set our young people's sights on the preservation of lives now lost to some form of dispute, famine, or disease every day, *right in our classrooms and living rooms*. The preventive diplomacy skills and case-study curriculum described in these three chapters will teach you how to do this, providing a blueprint for combining a rich, continuously updated, preventive diplomacy knowledge base with well-honed principles and practices of negotiation and conflict management and prevention, and how to deliver this in a hands-on, experiential role-playing manner that engages learners in many stages of development.

If, as the saying goes, the flutter of a butterfly's wing can trigger a chain of changes that creates a hurricane, the impact of these new lessons and ensuing experiences in preventive diplomacy is no less dramatic on a young person's development and her or his potential in the world. In the mind of a child at any age, these experiences of global interconnectedness have a profound effect, both at the time and over time. In the broader, global sense, the potential of one inspired human being is no small thing. And we have over 55 million school-age children in this country, so many of whom are eager to spread their wings, hungry for the chance to make a positive difference in the world.

It may seem odd, perhaps even presumptuous, to refer to US diplomatic training and kindergarten in the same sentence. I am not envisioning a diplomatic corps of five year olds being tutored to write foreign policy papers in Arabic or negotiate border treaties in Mandarin. I use the model of preventive diplomacy because I believe its principles provide an organizing theme and practical guide for upgrading and ultimately transforming every aspect of curriculum, from kindergarten through high school graduation and the transition to college and across the curriculum, from history to science to math to English courses. From a developmental point of view, children are natural experts on conflict. Conflicting ideas over who's in charge on the playground, or who gets what in the backyard (power and resources, respectively), or what a child has to do to get something else in return—these are all part of everyday family and school life. The principles and skills of conflict management and prevention have an even deeper foundation in normal child development. As children grow and mature, they naturally (and with our guidance) begin to see themselves in relation to others, they learn to collaborate for common gain or goodwill, and they learn—hopefully—to work out reasonable ways to settle differences. Not many children like a time-out. A two-year-old may grab a toy from a playmate or hit another child in a fit of anger. But as they grow, children's developing sense of empathy and fairness, their ability to manage their physical and emotional energy, and the brain development that enables them to learn and think in more complex ways naturally equip them for more thoughtful responses to their challenges and desires.

The effectiveness of personal conflict management and prevention training for children at every age has been well established in literature, how-to advice books, and education curricula such as "bullying prevention." The sixth grader who learns how to handle a conflict with a classmate over seating in the lunchroom or the ninth-grader who can learn to talk maturely through his frustration over an assignment with his teacher rather than act out or give up is acquiring, practicing, or developing fluency in important conflict management and prevention skills that they'll use throughout their lives.

And so much depends not only on what we teach them but also on *how* we teach them. How do we teach the seventeen year old who is pondering joining the Eight Tray (83) Gangster Crips in Los Angeles to think before acting or reacting? How do we get into the mind of the fifteen-year-old Palestinian boy brought up to martyr himself as a Hamas "cub" (or suicide bomber) in Jerusalem, or the child soldier in Somalia who is abducted from his family and trained to fight and kill for survival, to prevent him from killing others or himself? There are numerous examples of the open, willing nature of children to learn and be shaped by adults' expectations and instruction. If we fail to provide youth with better training for conflict management and prevention, then we leave them more vulnerable to training *for* conflict, to hurt themselves and others in order to be accepted.

What works in terms of conflict management and prevention training? Quite simply, hands-on, experiential, intellectual Outward Bound, conflict-resolution exercises that force students to focus on thorny issues that do not directly affect them—except by analogy. Students who learn about conflicts occurring in other areas worldwide by studying them—and communicating about them with peers in areas of conflict they are studying, via Skype—become more in-tune, street-smart global citizens as a result. With their own struggles seemingly at a safe distance, students get more involved as they are given the reins in negotiation simulations. Once they have analyzed the conflict in the case study and come up with creative ways to prevent future conflict in that particular area, they are asked to apply their new skills to preventing conflicts in their own communities and daily lives. Use of these exercises hundreds of times in middle and high schools around the United States and abroad has offered me proof of the lasting impact that the principles and practices of preventive diplomacy skills have on improving global IQ.

The Preventive Diplomacy Cheat Sheet: Principles and Practices

Preventive diplomacy eschews the "I win–you lose" negotiation style, also described as "positional bargaining," in which hard bargainers will do anything to win, and soft bargainers will give in to preserve the relationship. Neither leads to a fair, sustainable outcome. The more effective negotiation style for our purposes is "principled" or "integrative" bargaining, in which the bargainers search for workable ways to produce mutual benefits or gains for both sides. This win-win focus leads to more collaborative discussion, a more creative synthesis of ideas, and potentially innovative solutions for problems that previously appeared intractable.

While these concepts come from a variety of sources, one valuable book that I include in my teaching and require my Boston University students to read is *Getting to YES: Negotiating Agreement Without Giving In*, by Roger Fisher, William Ury, and Bruce Patton of the Harvard Negotiation Project. Fisher, who passed away in 2012, has been a particular inspiration, a longtime mentor who served as the keynote speaker when I launched my first international conflict prevention conference in June 2002 in Massachusetts. In creating preventive diplomacy principles and practices for students, I've drawn extensively from his and his colleagues' straightforward methods for negotiation and conflict resolution, specifically these four basic points: (1) separate the people from the problem; (2) focus on negotiating parties' interests, not positions; (3) invent options for mutual gain, not losses; and (4) agree to use objective criteria or standards, rather than vague ideas or outlines. Because students appreciate a light touch, a little humor, and some helpful alliteration (making things easier to remember), I've taken the collected wisdom of my mentors and packaged these principles and practices for teaching. My students call these the "mantras of our work in preventive diplomacy." I admit that I have been known to repeat them frequently. Every teacher knows, however, that repetition has a role in learning, and if a student leaves our work together with these mantras imbedded forever, it's a win-win.

Get Smart; Do the Homework

No one is an instant expert on anything. But even the most complex issues, from geopolitical issues like illegal immigration to thorny environmental issues like the efficacy of wind turbine electricity on Cape Cod, are open to inquiry and understanding. There is only one way to get smart about a subject or situation and that's to study it—on all sides, from every angle. First, I have my students read the historical background material and the chronology of events in a certain conflict. Second, I provide a chronology or time line of important events that have taken place over the history of the conflict. Then, I have them read a variety of news reports and commentaries by respected observers—and disrespected ones, as well. I teach students that extremists are rarely reticent. The other side in a negotiation may not be the extremists—they are often outlaws in their own societies—but the moderates must deal with them, they must live with them, and, unfortunately, they must at times die with them, too, if issues are not resolved effectively. I also provide students a glossary of important negotiation terms, a list of leaders involved in the conflict, and—most important—words and terms in the native languages of those involved. Remember the importance of becoming a chameleon? In this case, I teach students the importance of learning foreign languages of others when becoming skilled negotiators.

Walk in the Shoes of the Other Side

It's easy to say we should think about things from someone else's perspective, but it isn't always easy to do. In a case-study role-playing exercise, I ask students before the activity begins to identify which side they want to represent. For example, in the "Whose Jerusalem?" case study we will explore in the next chapter, I ask them if they would like to represent Likud (Israeli right-wing or conservative party members) or Hamas (the Palestinian extremist organization, with known political and terrorist wings). If a student indicates that she would like to be a Likud representative, she is surprised when I ask her to play the role of the opposite position, or Hamas, requiring her to learn, understand, and then defend the other side. This not only allows students to learn more about all sides of a conflict, but they also learn how to be more compassionate when arguing in favor of their original position. They tend to listen more carefully to all sides and learn the old diplomatic phrase, "We can at times agree to disagree," too. Finally, they learn that a vital diplomatic skill is to research and understand all sides in a conflict in order to attain more effectively what I identified above: "yes-yes" or mutual gains.

Separate the People from the Problem

I try to teach students what Fisher and Ury taught me: don't be hard on the other side. Doing so may completely derail negotiations, and it may ultimately prohibit the completion of a possible—albeit temporary—peace accord or successful conclusion to negotiations. "Be hard on the problem, but be easy on the people," was their important advice to me. One way to accomplish this in the middle or high school setting is to tell students that for those in the field of diplomacy, those who do the work of winning hearts and minds in negotiations, it is necessary to know that the person with whom you are negotiating also has a family, friends, interests, and amazing personal stories of love and loss. If you pay respect to the other side, memorizing names, birthplaces, and hobbies of your adversaries, if you treat the other side with respect, and if you smile often, instead of frowning and arguing, you gain much more respect from the other side in the long run. You see that the person with whom you are negotiating does not just possess the thoughts, ideas, and official positions of the other side's government or people. He or she possesses many of *your* personal thoughts, ideas, and positions that you deem close to your heart. Hence, I tell my students to study the person or persons with whom they will be negotiating, walking in their shoes before negotiations, making an effort to understand the personal interests and language and culture of the other side's representative. Can you imagine the look on the face of a Palestinian negotiator when, as an American, you enter the room saying *Salam wa aleikum* (Peace), asking how her husband and four children are, and offering a cup of mint tea, a favorite of my Palestinian friends?

Focus on Interests, not Positions

Positions from the outset are defined points of view that negotiators hope to defend at the negotiation table. In negotiating over the future status of Jerusalem, for example, Israeli and Palestinian leaders will often haggle over positions such as: "Israeli security in and around Jerusalem is vital to prevent future suicide bombings," "Palestinian sovereignty over the heart of Old Jerusalem is crucial," or "The expansion of Israeli settlements in East Jerusalem will continue for years and years to come." The problem with positions, however, is that they create yes-or-no obstacles. The talented negotiator does not allow positions to create obstacles, but rather seeks to define each side's interests. Interests present problems to be solved, in creative ways. For example, although Palestinians and Israelis—or students playing the roles of these key stakeholders in the Middle East conflict during a negotiation simulation exercise—may not share the same faith, all of the negotiators can work together, asking questions such as, "What would you think if we were to work together to create a calendar for the next twelve months, during which time, if there are no more suicide bombings, an East Jerusalem settlement expansion freeze will be put in place?" This is a question based on a mutual interest—an end to suicide bombing and the creation of new living space—not the proclamation of a position. And it empowers both sides in negotiations, for it is a question that both sides may answer, taking part in dialogue.

Pay Attention to Body Language

Learn more than proper grammar in negotiations. Positioning at the negotiation table and proper body language are important, too. Are the negotiators far from each other across a table, or are they working side by side? Are they leaning in physically, demonstrating interest and active participation in the negotiating process or are they disengaged, leaning back in the chair? Or are they doing so simply to listen? And if they are disengaged in some way, might they become even more disengaged, with legs crossed, arms crossed, and hands over their mouths? These could be red flags indicating that negotiations are not proceeding well.

Learn How to Talk So People Will Listen

In addition to body language, the choice of words and tone of voice are crucial diplomatic tools to be refined before going to the negotiating table. Expressions such as "I greatly appreciate your thoughts" and "I respect your position" are excellent ways to begin productive dialogue.

SILENCE. As I am fond of saying, "*Listen* spelled another way is *silent.*" Do you show respect to the other side in negotiations by remaining silent and listening often? The Greek philosopher Epictetus told us that "we have two ears and one mouth, so that we can listen twice as much as we speak." This means that you must learn to listen much more than you speak in negotiations to improve the possibility that you will achieve a positive resolution to the conflict.

TONE. When you speak, are you able to establish easy two-way communications so that your negotiating relationship is—from the outset—not adversarial? While you are negotiating, are you screaming or yelling, raising your voice, or arguing? Are you negotiating with a firm yet respecting tone, or are you whispering? Are you speaking in an arrogant manner? Or are you speaking in a humble way?

WORD CHOICE. Do you use the imperative (or command) form of verbs in stating your demands? For example, do you say, "Give me this specific piece of land!" Or do you use the first person plural ("we") pronoun or verb to soften your presentation of the argument (a "we are working together" idea), in order to work on a mutual-gains agreement? For example: "Might we speak about this specific piece of land in order to ascertain who might be willing to give what in terms of land holdings and occupation?" Instead of using the imperative form of verbs while engaged in negotiations, why not use the conditional tense and phrase it as a question? For example: "Would you be willing to speak about a freeze of expanded construction of housing on this specific piece of land in order to ascertain who might be willing to give what in terms of a freeze in violence there?"

Go for the Win-Win

In this part of negotiations, the good negotiator must help both—or multiple—sides draft commitments they *all* agree to, creating what Fisher and Ury call "mutual gains" in negotiations, so that leaders on both or all sides are able to achieve some, if not all, of their goals without compromising the interests of their own constituents, working together to create options that will satisfy all parties. Negotiators often offer little, demand much, and stubbornly haggle over a single quantifiable issue like money, as if they are in a bazaar trying to talk a merchant down in terms of his or her price for a certain product. And in addition, diplomatic officials are under political pressure to be inflexible and not generate options that are good for both sides, because they can be criticized or chastised upon their return home.

Know Your BATNA—and Know Theirs

BATNA is the Fisher and Ury acronym for "best alternative to a negotiated agreement." It is an established term in negotiations parlance and, in its simplest terms, represents the best offer you can make if you conclude that negotiating with a particular party is not likely to yield anything more favorable. You can walk away from a negotiation if your BATNA is better than the likely outcome of that negotiation; it may be your plan B, C, or D, but it is more than you had before you came to the negotiating table.

In the "Whose Jerusalem?" case study, middle and high school students learn through hands-on negotiation practice just how important it is for an excellent negotiator to have a BATNA for such matters as how to divide the capital, Jerusalem, in terms of settlement expansion (or not) and sovereignty over the Old City. In these negotiations, students representing the Israeli Likud Party know that the most radical members of Hamas would like to control the entire city of Jerusalem, including West and East Jerusalem and the Old City, dear to Christians, Muslims, and Jews alike. The BATNA for the arch-strategist Likud party members: to offer Hamas, in the first round of negotiations, two outlying suburbs in East Jerusalem as their new capital. When this proposal is quickly declined by members of Hamas, what is the BATNA? Members of Likud come back to the negotiation table and offer Hamas all of East Jerusalem, the Christian and Muslim quarters, as their new capital, but declare that Israelis will maintain sovereignty over West Jerusalem and the Old City, offering Palestinians only custodianship over the Old City, something, as Likud members explain, that the King of Saudi Arabia has over the two other religious sites most important to Muslims: Mecca and Medina.

This knowledge of alternatives reflects excellent negotiation strategies, as well as improved critical thinking, creativity, and collaboration skills. In fact, the underlying principle of BATNA is already at work in other ways: when students strategize how to study, for example. Just as land resources are not infinite, neither is a student's time. Should they do an extra credit project well with hopes of boosting a semester grade by one point, or study for a long time for the final exam that's worth 25 percent of the semester grade? In a world where there is no perfect solution, much of life is a negotiation, and students are always delighted to discover they are natural strategists and that the skills they are using in everyday school life have a place in the larger scheme of things, including how they understand global affairs.

Peace Is a Process, Not a Prize

There is no such thing as a lasting peace. Peace isn't something you achieve and then leave behind as if it were a framed treaty on a wall, assuming that attaining peace is a completed task that will last for decades to come. Peace is a continuing process of conversation and interaction. There is no lasting peace, but there is sustainable peace, achieved through an ongoing process of communication, comprehension, critical thinking, compromise, collaboration, creativity, compassion, and—one hopes—more stable coexistence. In a case-study simulation exercise, as in the UN, all sides must learn and practice working jointly, peacefully, and continually on what will be an endless stream of differences, a peace "process." Jointly, all sides must begin by devising an architect's model of the problem, defining all of the facets of the conflict. Then, they must create an initial architect's model of the problems. The process can be envisioned as an architectural and engineering project that is drafted together, discussed, and refined again and again, before it is finally built in the form of a peace treaty. Then, as I always tell students, days or years or months later, this beautifully crafted peace model can and must continue to be remodeled.

Every student has the makings of an expert negotiator. The developmental progress we observe as students move from a child's selfish "gimme" mentality and into the more complex "What do I have to do to get it?" strategic thinking of adolescence readies them for the next step toward becoming enlightened global citizens with improved global IQ. Granted, that next step—comprehending other peoples' situations, perceptions, and motives—may for some still be only a primitive self-serving adaptation of the "gimme" mentality (even in some adults). But for most students, it opens the door for a genuine step forward in learning. How have I seen this applied by students?

Imagine two high school seniors, the president and vice president of their class. It is spring of senior year. They have already been accepted to college, early decision. They are leading the planning committee for the graduation ceremony and would like to order Class of

2012 T-shirts for all class members, with all of their names on the shirts, too. Because they have procrastinated, they quickly arrange a meeting with a T-shirt manufacturer's sales representative. When he arrives, he tells the two that he would be able to complete the task—for $18 per T-shirt. Stunned, the two seniors declare that they thought the price would be no more than $10 per shirt. The sales rep realizes that they are desperate and sticks with the price of $18 per T-shirt. Because they need to have the shirts available for graduation, the seniors agree, feeling guilty about the price tag.

Now, imagine those same two seniors, in the *fall* of their senior year. They search for T-shirt prices for a senior class of 275 students, find competitive prices, and then they call the same sales rep. When he introduces the $18 price, they believe that he will stick with that price because the shirts are of high quality. The students' BATNA and better negotiation position with this sales rep is that they have already set up a meeting later in the week with another sales rep whom they think will offer a better price. Those students know about BATNA and how to improve their bargaining position to get what they hope will be a lower T-shirt price from this sales rep.

Young people are often surprised to learn that the negotiation strategies that are key to "getting to yes" in everyday life are the same ones that international experts in diplomacy use in sophisticated, multinational circumstances, negotiating for life-and-death stakes in troubled regions. They are surprised to think of themselves as potentially valuable contributors to creating conditions for peaceful coexistence in their lifetime. But in truth, with their fresh perspective, energy, technological savvy, and innovative out-of-the-box thinking, these students should and can develop their own basic skills in negotiation, and practice them as well. When students look at the world through the lens of negotiation to prevent conflict—or preventive diplomacy—they see the possibilities to prevent myriad conflicts more effectively in their own lives today and perhaps in their own or other countries years from now, and their faces light up. In the next chapter, you will be able to see them come to attention in their seats, both physically and mentally, when we put these principles and practices into action.

CHAPTER SIX

The Case Study in Action

Role-Play for Peace

I had devoted years of my life to teaching conflict resolution before I decided there rarely is such a thing. At least not in the way we imagine it. In the global arena especially, where the causes of war, violence, and conflict have such deep roots (in historic, religious, political, economic, and social inequities and injustices), resolving a conflict often doesn't make it go away forever. As long as the root causes remain—or memories of the conflict have yet to heal—the potential for conflict is constant and real.

As a result, I decided while studying at the Tufts Fletcher School between 1991 and 1993 that we must teach middle and high school students how to examine these conflicts and to simulate effective management and prevention of the conflicts—preventive diplomacy, in other words—in a long and vital process. The process I have attempted to refine for almost twenty years follows a carefully refined pedagogical sequence that goes from the initial student engagement with a topic ("What exactly is the Arab-Israeli conflict?"), through even-handed teacher- and student-led dialogue about the issue, to debate and negotiation, and ultimately to a conclusion that includes—and this is vitally important—how the conflict and other conflicts like it could be managed and prevented more effectively in the minds of students collaborating creatively in classrooms across the United States and around the world on the issue. This process can be compressed into the space of a fifty-minute class period, a one-day workshop, or—as in real-world talks—weeks, months, or years. The general steps are as follows:

- *Research* (information gathering). Teach students, for example, what the history of the Arab-Israeli conflict is.
- *Review and evaluation.* Teach students how to review historical information, brainstorm, analyze, and plan negotiations over one specific point; for example, the possible division of Jerusalem, or the creation of a Palestinian state.
- *Discussion.* Talk about the initial face-to-face engagement and media literacy; evaluate media coverage of the issue from many different news sources that portray the subject very differently: Al Jazeera, the *Jerusalem Post*, the *New York Times*, CNN, Fox, the BBC. Have a conceptual dialogue about how various news sources depict the story.
- *Negotiation.* Describe and oversee specific negotiations, focusing on the issue and employing Fisher and Ury's *Getting to Yes* strategies.
- *Conclusion.* Give the topic *meaning* by having students author a sharp, focused position paper signed by each of them and sent to powerful people: for example, President Barack Obama; Secretary of State Hillary Rodham Clinton; and Massachusetts senator John Kerry, chair of the Senate Foreign Relations Committee.

How can we possibly communicate this valuable pedagogical process of preventive diplomacy, which I often call an art or a subtle, skillful handling of complex situations, in the time periods allotted in the normal school calendar? How can we teach the key principles introduced in the last chapter in a way that will quickly engage students and turn a complex subject of study into an immediate hands-on learning experience? The answer is by using what I call an "intellectual Outward Bound" case study, focused on one particular geopolitical conflict, so that students can take part in what I call a "role-play for peace" exercise in which I give them an exciting piece of the action. A case study can be developed into role-playing by expanding the five general steps presented above into eight distinct phases. These phases are (1) individual preparation, (2) prenegotiation team meetings, (3) negotiations—round one, (4) team consultation and revisit strategy, (5) negotiations—round two, (6) negotiations—round three, (7) negotiations—round four, (8) negotiations—final round, and (9) agreement and 250-word position paper, or BATNA (best alternative to a negotiated agreement, from Fisher and Ury's, *Getting to Yes*), and adjournment.

One of my conflict-resolution case studies in its simplest definition is a bound, written document that introduces a long-standing political, social, economic, or religious conflict, or a seemingly intractable cultural dilemma, to students in an understandable manner. It might focus on the Arab-Israeli conflict, as I mentioned before. The case study described here, "Whose Jerusalem?" focuses on the future of Jerusalem, a very important, divided holy city that is one of the major flashpoints in the continuing Israeli-Palestinian conflict. Another case study deals with AIDS in Sub-Saharan Africa (the case study: "We SAID AIDS!"—the word "SAID" standing for "South Africa's Invisible Death"). Another case study focuses on the problems facing Rwanda eighteen years after the height of the genocide that killed nearly eight hundred thousand people in one hundred days and is entitled "Rwanda: Reconciliation and Reconstruction, or Return to Conflict?" Other case studies deal with illegal immigration in the United States, the phenomenon of date rape in our local communities, and other hot-button issues. (For a complete list of Axis of Hope case studies, see the resources section at the back of this book.)

The important elements in each case study are that there are several understandable and relatively short chapters in each: (1) the history of the conflict; (2) a chronology providing students with important dates in the conflict, or an understandable time line of events; (3) a glossary of important people, places, and terms in the different languages of the conflicting sides (examples: Benjamin Netanyahu, Mahmoud Abbas, Jerusalem, jihad, intifada, chutzpah); and (4) six distinct yet integral viewpoints or key players in the conflict scenario that the participating students must represent. In the "Whose Jerusalem?" case study, for instance, the six parties (grouped into three pairs by overlapping interests) are Hamas (led by Ismail Haniyeh) and Fatah (led by Mahmoud Abbas [Abu Mazem]), the Israeli Labor Party (led by Shelly Yechimovich) and Israeli Likud Party (led by Benjamin Netanyahu), and representatives of the Arab League and of the Quartet (the latter being a supranational group that includes the United Nations, the United States, the European Union, and Russia). Having these pairs placed at each of the three points on a triangle creates what I call "diplomatic triangulation": the ability to perceive common ground between opposite poles.

"Whose Jerusalem?" The Case Study in Action

At one workshop I directed at an independent school in Sarasota, Florida, the Out-of-Door Academy, sixty-five students gathered for a daylong workshop in the school library using the "Whose Jerusalem?" case study to learn about the Arab-Israeli conflict, the art of negotiation, and preventive diplomacy. After introductory comments to the group, we moved to the activities that, in real-world diplomatic terms, are described as icebreakers, team-building and confidence-building exercises gleaned over the years from Outward Bound, the National Outdoor Leadership School (NOLS), and YMCA/YWCA. In real-life state negotiations, trust can take years to cultivate, with activities ranging from formal dinners to ongoing formal meetings among top-tier diplomats to live videoconferences in a host of languages. But in the conflict management and prevention world, it is crucial.

Hence, as we only had one day for our Sarasota workshop, we needed to establish trust quickly, so we began with some fun exercises. This is when students I have worked with around the world get to know one another by name, feel comfortable with one another, and begin to develop the skills of engagement, focus, and team play that are needed for the effective conflict management and prevention teamwork exercises that are to follow. They also learn in subtle ways that they share many interests, from common names to common birthdays to common preferences, from ice cream flavors to television programs and films to world leaders they admire. In short, this is a proven way to effectively build "interest connections" before students begin learning to negotiate.

The Sarasota students arrive in the meeting room, find seats, and are just settling in when I give them their first instruction: "Would we stand up, please?" (Notice that I ask them a question using the first person plural "we," empowering them to listen, think, and decide.) I point to the wall on my left and the wall on my right, and ask them to form a straight line by first names, in alphabetical order, starting with A on the left wall—"If you are an Aaron, you are over there"—and ending with Z on the right wall—"If you are a Zoe, you are against that wall." And then I say, "But one minute, please. What is the word *listen* spelled another way?" Very few know the answer. So, I state, "*Listen* spelled another way is *silent*, and both of these words represent crucial skills in the field of diplomacy." This exercise must be done silently, without saying a word, and they have one minute to form the perfect "name line" in alphabetical order. I look at my watch and give them the signal to start. What happens next is magical. Those students, with no apparent fear, start forming the shapes of letters with their hands or their arms. What is so amazing is that they do so in a way that is understandable to the students looking at them (forming, for example, a backward letter *c* to themselves, as if they *know* how to make it more understandable to the other person) to indicate which people should go where. Others who find that they have the same first names immediately realize that they should consider the first letter of the last name or simply stand side by side.

"Ten more seconds!" I say, as the clock runs out. They are turbocharged to finish forming the alphabetical name line quickly. When the minute is up, they freeze in place, and then, from the far left "A" wall to the far right "Z" wall, I ask each student to say her or his name clearly so we can all learn them, including me, knowing that remembering names is extremely important in diplomacy and in teaching, too. The exercise is more than just fun. It is an icebreaker experience of communication and the role of body language as an important form of nonverbal communication and a valuable tool in negotiations as well.

Once we have completed this silent introduction exercise (another option is to ask them to silently arrange themselves in order of birthdays, without including the year), students are relaxed and happy to learn that the next exercise includes talking—and ice cream. Or at least talking about ice cream, along with other favorite things. I pick a category—favorite ice cream flavor, movie, television show, band, or singer, and so on—and ask them to name their favorite of each and group together with others who share that preference.

Immediately, the students with leader instincts begin looking around the room and stating in loud voices: "Chocolate over here!" Or "Oreo Mint Chip over here!" Other students, instead of yelling the flavor, are listening for their favorite flavor to be called out so they can identify the group with which they belong, and they rush over to join their ice cream–flavor peers. Then, after just one minute, I go around the room asking each group what their flavor is. The answers tell about more than ice cream. At times, the leader who gathered the group plays the role of spokesperson and tells the rest of us the flavor. But often, the whole group responds together excitedly, at times even hugging one another (or, if it is a group of boys, high-fiving) as they do so. And some, interestingly enough, stand alone, self-confident enough to be able to state that they prefer a certain type of ice cream even though nobody else does, or that they don't have a favorite flavor, or that they are lactose intolerant!

My "find your group" questions become progressively more serious, such as "Who is your favorite US president in our nation's history?" or "Who is your favorite 2012 presidential candidate?" Or one that foreshadows the negotiations ahead and reflecting a real present-day crisis: "Given the increasing tensions in the Middle East, and the talks over the creation of the State of Palestine with pre-1967 Six-Day War borders, are you pro-Palestinian, pro-Israeli, or something else?" Why is this exercise important? Because these students, who may become "allies" or "enemies" as they begin negotiations later in the day, have already learned that, whatever comes up in that tense environment of negotiations, they have many other interests in common.

Other exercises include "trust falls" in which one student falls into the collective arms of two students standing behind. In another favorite, I have each group that will be representing a political party in the negotiations come together in a tight circle. Each first reaches out with the right hand to grasp the right hand of another member of the group; next each reaches out with the left hand and grasps the left hand of another member. Then they all try to get themselves out of this incredible knot they have just created, which is possible only if everyone works together toward a common goal. Finally, I have them place their left shoulders into the center of the circle as closely together as possible. I then ask, "What do you create when you sit down?" When there is silence, I say: "A lap, which becomes the seat for the person in front of you." I then ask them, on the count of three, to sit down. After two to three tries, inevitably the students learn as a team to support one another (by holding on to the shoulder of the person in front of her or him, for example) and to succeed at this exercise. All the exercises are designed to have students learn through physical experience, take calculated risks, trust, and work as a team to overcome obstacles.

After this, we engage in several exercises that bring them more directly in touch with some of the underlying issues of conflict: turf battles and scarce resources. This is a version of an Outward Bound "ropes course," but there is no rope climbing. In the first exercise, using a long yellow rope, I make a small outline of a map of Israel, the West Bank, the Gaza Strip, and the Golan Heights, on the floor. I then ask each group taking part in the "Whose Jerusalem?" negotiation exercise (Likud, Labor, Hamas, Fatah, Arab League, and the Quartet) to send three representatives to "fit" into the outlined map I have created on the floor. I then remind the Palestinian groups—extremists and moderates alike—that they occupy the Gaza Strip and a portion of the West Bank, in refugee camps there, locations of which they must determine with the other parties already inside the yellow rope. I instruct them to keep their feet and their hands inside the rope, with no part of their bodies touching the floor outside it. Given the size of the map I've created, this is a nearly impossible task. While the students are struggling, I ask them questions: "Who is living in a 'Palestinian refugee camp'? And who is living in an 'Israeli settlement'? Who are 'right wingers'? And who are 'extremists'? Who are 'terrorists' and who are 'freedom fighters'?" This exercise teaches students how difficult even a simple territorial dispute can be and how to come up with creative solutions to problems of fragile coexistence. One group, for example, did not stand side by side in order to "occupy" more of a particular area. Instead, they got on the shoulders of other members of their groups to create a supportive way to allow more to live there. Others quickly learned to lock arms across the circle (as in the "circle sit" exercise) to support one another so that they didn't fall out of the small, enclosed area of the map.

In the second exercise, outdoors and usually on a school football field, I place the yellow rope along the fifty-yard line. I then place the two pro-Israeli groups (Likud and Labor) on one side of the field and pro-Palestinian groups (Hamas and Fatah) on the other side. I allow members of the Quartet and the Arab League groups to choose which side to go to. Then I take half of the Likud members and half of the Hamas members and place them in the "jails," or the two end zones behind the opposite sides' goal line. The rules are announced (a variety of the game of tag or "Jailbreak"): "The only way to achieve freedom is for members of your team to cross the middle opposition line (or cross over the fifty-yard line) and go all the way to the opposite end zone, tagging your jailed compatriots in the opposite end zone to free them. If this is achieved, the person who had been in jail and the person who freed him or her have a free right of passage to return to their side of the field." Then I end it saying, "This practice in team building, team loyalty, and risk taking will prove useful later when you must think on your feet at the negotiation table."

Preparations Begin in Earnest

After these high-energy icebreaker and team-building exercises, students return to the main conference room, which becomes a hub of quiet activity as each student finds a computer terminal and settles in for a forty-five-minute electronic briefing. In phase one, individual preparation includes studying a wide variety of that day's online articles about the Arab-Israeli conflict—Benjamin Netanyahu's meeting in the Oval Office with President Obama, for example, or presidential candidate Mitt Romney's visit to Israel—as well as historical documents, such as the reasons behind the 1967 Six-Day War. Students can also send themselves e-mails before beginning their conflict-resolution role-play exercises, with several newspaper and magazine article links that offer them opposing views of the Palestinian-Israeli conflict and the role the United States has or has not played in ending it. (This in itself is an important exercise in media literacy, discussed in chapter 3.) Before the workshop begins, students might also read excerpts from *Getting to Yes* (discussed in the previous chapter), or former President Jimmy Carter's *Talking Peace: A Vision for the Next Generation*. Or they might watch Oliver Stone's powerful documentary, *Persona Non Grata*, about the Palestinian-Israeli conflict and one of the bloodiest rounds of Mideast violence that began in September 2000.

In the case of the Sarasota students, once they complete their historical background readings about the Palestinian-Israeli conflict and study of an in-depth chronology of the conflict, they receive a glossary of terms, a list of important names, and their role-play assignments. Each conference participant gets a different colored, confidential four-page briefing on the role he or she will play as a member of a team: again, the six sides—a member of Hamas, Fatah, Israeli Likud, or Israeli Labor, or a representative of the Quartet or Arab League, the latter two groups acting as moderators overseeing the negotiation process. These confidential briefings explain their groups' positions and the limits to which students will be able to go in negotiating the division of Jerusalem.

These roles are not necessarily those that conference participants chose when they handed in a piece of paper that morning on which they wrote their choice of role. I often assign them to different groups, forcing them to walk in others' shoes and defend a side they might not necessarily agree with. This ability is at the heart of being a good negotiator or leader. I call it "the Tom Brady edge." Just as New England Patriots' star quarterback Tom Brady studies other NFL teams' defenses for hours before playing against them to figure out how best to defeat them, a good negotiator knows how to get into the minds of and adopt the ideas and strategies of all sides prior to commencing negotiations.

After participants have been briefed individually on their roles, they review my checklist based on the principles of preventive diplomacy (presented in the previous chapter). This reminder, the "Six Elements of Negotiation," helps players identify trouble spots and strategies to keep the talks on track.

1. Are there poor communications? Establish better two-way communications. These can include listening more effectively, taking careful written notes, and asking questions to clarify points of uncertainty.

2. Is the negotiation relationship adversarial? Build a better side-by-side working relationship. Literally, think about negotiating next to instead of across the table from representatives of the other side. Also, think about placing representatives of both sides in an "A, B, A, B, and so on" setting with no table in the middle, creating less of an us-versus-them scenario, and more transparency without a table.

3. Are interests ignored? Are there too few options? Learn all interests, on all sides. When focusing on Jerusalem, begin by asking the representatives of the group that your group is negotiating with to work on individual lists of priorities (security, settlement expansion, and so on) and then methodically discuss them, attempting to learn about possible commonalities. Jointly invent new and creative options, taking into consideration all interests.

4. Are there no persuasive standards of fairness in how to negotiate? Teach students to brainstorm about and find standards of fairness persuasive to both. These might include who speaks first and for how long, or if, when meeting, students may speak to representatives at other negotiating tables.

5. Are commitments uncertain? Teach students that building trust is very important during negotiations. Draft commitments they

want—and those they can offer in writing and refine constantly during negotiations.

6. And, finally, what's your bottom line? Always know your BATNA and carefully estimate the BATNA of the other side as well.

The Case Study Takes Off

The negotiation strategies I share with students are straightforward and easy to learn. But I have to honestly tell them that in the art of negotiation, these strategies are not always perfect. From decades of study and work in the field of negotiation and preventive diplomacy, I have come to understand that although solutions to global conflicts—such as treaties—can only come about through long, often tenuous rounds of negotiation, the process of negotiation is often imperfect. The process involves human frailty and anger, while at the same time requiring that decisions that will affect one person—or an entire country—are made too often very quickly. But to give up on negotiations essentially means abandoning future prospects of peace, and for most of us in this fragile world, that is not an acceptable option.

In phase two, prenegotiation team meetings, the six Sarasota teams (Hamas, Fatah, and so on) hold separate, simultaneous meetings around their individual tables to get to know each other, plan strategies, and devise the group's two-minute summary statement that will be read to all the groups. They also decide on data needs, they must choose a spokesperson and secretary, and more. Many teachers of conflict resolution, like me, feel that these initial team meetings can often be the most difficult round of negotiations, prior to talks with other sides in the conflict. Why? Because they must decide very quickly how to agree on the content of the two-minute summary and what positions they, as a cohesive team, will take in later rounds of negotiations.

Following this planning period, which is an important team-building exercise in diplomacy, each group's spokesperson stands up and, in no more than two minutes, offers his or her group's summary statement. In Sarasota, as I often do, I have the moderate groups share their summary statements first (Arab League and Quartet). I then move to the more centrist groups' summary statements (Fatah and Labor Party) and finish with the more radical, hard-line positions (Hamas and Likud). It is amazing to see how students take on these roles and feel empowered while doing so, even though they might not agree with the position their side is taking on the future of Jerusalem. This is when they begin to say to themselves, "Wow. We are actually able to make decisions by ourselves, and to present these to others. We no longer have to memorize and regurgitate information given to us by adults." This is when the intellectual light bulbs—and the glow of self-confidence—begin to shine.

In phase three, the first round of negotiations begins. Members of Hamas meet with members of Fatah, Arab League representatives meet with members of the Quartet, and Israeli Likud party members meet with Israeli Labor Party members. It is useful to break negotiations into small, digestible groups or what I call "diplomatic pods" and focus on a small, fixed set of issues to discuss. During the first round of the negotiations, each pair of negotiating parties discusses three issues concerning Jerusalem: present and future security of the city; continued Israeli settlement expansion in East Jerusalem or not; and the question of control—or "sovereignty"—over Old Jerusalem and the holy sites, including the Western Wall (or Wailing Wall) and Temple Mount (*Har haBáyith* in Hebrew and *Haram Ash-Sharif* in Arabic, both important languages students are exposed to in this exercise). Typically there is a great deal of tension and there are some attempts to be positional on these important issues. Early optimists predicting easy agreement are inevitably proved wrong.

In Sarasota on this exciting day of formal negotiations, one normally introverted ninth-grade Jewish student speaks out passionately against the oppression of her people—playing the role of a Hamas Party member incredibly well. In character, she demands a political and economic stake in Jerusalem and promises an end to the suicide bombings—as long as Palestinians are given the quality health care, educational systems, and political voices that they deserve. This same girl, two years before, had her bat mitzvah in Jerusalem. Another bright girl, representing the Quartet, sees tempers flaring among other groups; as a result, she asks me if she can dash between them with small notes, intending to orchestrate compromises via "shuttle diplomacy." I immediately say yes. Meanwhile, a boy whose devoutly Jewish parents were not in favor of his participation in these negotiation exercises, plays the role of a Likud Party member. Claiming to be a dear friend and confidant of Israeli prime minister Benjamin Netanyahu, he declares that he and his party will walk out of the negotiations if they are even asked to meet with the terrorist organization Hamas.

In phase four, consulting and revisiting strategy, the teams take a time-out to individually regroup and prepare and then present short summaries of their refined positions, following the first round of negotiations, to all assembled. As each group reads its summary statements, all the other groups listen carefully, take notes, and look for possible bargaining chips to use in later rounds. Individual delegations then regroup to see if any new progress has been made in light of the first round, the summaries, or any interventions, such as one offered by the Quartet member who had been racing between groups. Interventions are also something like a wild card in a conventional game, which can include any of the following:

- Conference facilitators like me may make up-to-the-minute news announcements about what is happening that day, in Jerusalem or in the Mideast, to make negotiations more real, difficult, and complex.

- Any delegation may issue statements in response to these announcements or as early olive-branch measures to other groups they are meeting with at the same time or will be meeting with later.

- Per the news announcements, so-called spoilers on any side in the negotiations can take or deny responsibility for acts of violence that have been reported.

- At this point, any delegation may announce its reaction to these events.
- Any delegation may also request a consultation meeting with any other, or among its own members alone.

In phase five, round two of negotiations opens with newly assigned pairs of groups meeting together for the first time. They continue to focus on the future of Jerusalem, and the three issues I introduced above: security, settlement expansion, and sovereignty. They may set forth new questions, agendas, and goals. Although this is a carefully orchestrated negotiation simulation, the tensions and frustrations experienced by participants are very real, as emotionally charged students take over the negotiation process, as well as their personal learning processes, once again. In Sarasota, one student, playing the role of a Fatah Party member, asserts: "We demand that the Netanyahu government cease construction of new Israeli settlements in East Jerusalem and that the Israeli army leave that part of the city at once, and grant control of that area to the Palestinian Authority, immediately." "No, we cannot accept your proposal for security reasons," responds another student playing the role of Israel's right-wing Likud Party. "However, we are willing to allow gradually increasing movement for Palestinians in the city's holy sites, including Temple Mount, with implementation dates to be set immediately."

At one point during negotiations, student-led talks nearly break down as several participants discuss whether Israeli settlers living in or near East Jerusalem who were suspected of crimes should be tried in Israeli or Palestinian courts. One student, playing an Israeli Likud Party member, threatens to end negotiations if settlers are not allowed to be tried uniquely in the Israeli court system. "If they're not tried in Israeli courts, the negotiations are over, period," he proclaims, as his fist slams down on the table.

Statements such as these volley across the negotiation tables over the course of the entire day, as participating students become key stakeholders in this fragile Middle East peace process. They might not agree with the strong, politically charged words coming out of their own mouths, but their assignment is to understand the complexity of the Middle East conflict by fighting passionately for the interests of the people they represent. And to their credit, they learn a great deal about the art of negotiation—and compromise—in only one day of seeking to divide the holy city of Jerusalem, an incredibly complex and challenging task.

In phases six and seven, negotiations continue, as pairs of delegations are changed each time and are asked to start obtaining—and documenting—any concessions or proposals made by this group, which could be announced to the other parties that are meeting.

In phase eight, drafting a position paper marks a break in traditional negotiations. Now, the six teams, given a clear time limit of thirty-minutes, must generate a 250-word peace agreement. How? First, each group is asked to meet individually once again, as they had done earlier in the day, to author their two-minute summary statements. This time, each of the six groups will have to divide themselves into three smaller groups, each of which will go to one of three tables: one table will focus on the future of security in Jerusalem, another on East Jerusalem settlements, and the third on sovereignty in the Old City. In this final round of negotiations, each of the six sides is thus represented at each table, at which an idea or goal—not the defense of a party and its ideas—is the focus. This is the "focus on interests, not positions," discussed in the previous chapter. Figuring out which one-third of each group will go to which table helps students organize their thoughts regarding progress made and steps to take in creating their final 250-word position paper. And it will give them the power to draft the paper, focusing on the proposed future of Jerusalem. In its final draft, the paper, like all those generated by these conferences, is then sent to President Barack Obama, Secretary of State Hillary Rodham Clinton, Special Envoy for Middle East Peace David Hale, and Senate Foreign Relations Committee Chairman John F. Kerry.

The particular agreement that the students craft after one, two, or three days of intense negotiations could realistically never be brokered that quickly. Yet the negotiation process has been realistic enough to give students an experience of the high-pressure, high-stakes, emotion-packed arena of international conflict-resolution summit conferences, and a starter set of negotiation skills they could perhaps use someday in such a context to deal effectively with international geopolitical conflicts and other complex conflicts that they may encounter.

As one Sarasota conference attendee put it:

> You can go to class and learn mathematics and science and English, all important disciplines, don't get me wrong. But something like this, the complex Arab-Israeli conflict, is something that is going on in the real world, in the lives of our counterparts in the Middle East. And I think that we need to start learning to deal with these conflicts because they have not yet been solved—and they will never go away. We really need to begin to find a solution to global problems like these—beginning today.

When Global Intelligence Becomes Global Responsibility

What does this all mean? Passionate, self-motivated students were exhausted after the case-study-based exercise I oversaw in Sarasota, intellectually, emotionally, and physically. But they also became transformed and empowered by participating actively in this experience, not simply listening to lectures, memorizing facts, and regurgitating this information on tests or exams. In practicing the art of negotiation firsthand, they develop a more profound understanding of the Arab-Israeli conflict along with what I call "international street smarts." And as they begin to comprehend more profoundly the lives, cultures, religions, and histories of others, they learn to hone their skills of critical thinking, effective oral and written communication, creativity, collaboration, agility, adaptation, social and diplomatic innovation, compromise, and more peaceful coexistence in their own lives as well. This is where a feeling of global responsibility takes root.

In follow-up letters and e-mails from the Sarasota participants, they describe the case-study role-play as a truly transformative experience:

> Before I heard about the program coming to our school, I admit I was extremely unaware of the conflict that was taking place over the division of Jerusalem. I took part in the program at first just to learn about that, and, well . . . to be completely honest I discovered a whole other world. Recently I've become a news junkie and I am more culturally aware, which I believe I must credit your program for. I can't thank you enough for coming to our school and opening my eyes. I hope everything is going well and you continue to enlighten others like me.

> The conference really brought home the multifaceted Middle Eastern conflict, and the challenges of finding a solution that provides for everyone's happiness and coexistence. The work you are doing is often overlooked, as "short-term solutions" are sought, but I learned there is no quick fix, and the more our generation learns about the problems we will inherit, the better.

> First, I just want to thank you for coming to our school and allowing me and the other students a chance to see the Palestinian-Israeli conflict outside of the biases that are offered by the media. Nowadays it is easy to build yourself a box and stay confined to a routine. I can easily say that the Axis of Hope conference broke down whatever barriers of routine that I had, and brought the outside world and conflicts into brilliant clarity.

From their comments, it is clear that for each, the deeply affecting aspect of our time together couldn't be boiled down to just one thing. It wasn't that these middle and high school students had never cared about other people or other cultures and that suddenly their social conscience had been awakened. Nor was it only that the case-study material had opened their eyes to the historical and current context for a particular geopolitical conflict. Or that the role-play had been fun and engaging or that it had taught them negotiation skills they could see applications for in their own lives. It was the sum and synthesis of all those elements, a delicate balancing act that, when organized well and overseen with focus and passion, can completely change students' views of the world. There is something galvanizing in the process, something in the combination of ideas, activity, and purpose. There is also an aligning of the stars: the stars of exploration, passion, focus, maturity, purpose, and compassion, all coming together above students in their formative years to create something they will never forget, and that we should contemplate recreating in all classrooms and dining rooms across the United States.

The "Whose Jerusalem?" case study has been presented in schools worldwide, in varied settings and with students and faculty who bring with them diverse backgrounds, abilities, and points of view. One setting was a Chicago inner-city public high school where many students attending are gang members. Here, for two days, I was asked to use the exercise as a conflict management and prevention course in an intense session with formerly incarcerated youth, many of them from rival gangs. It was at times difficult for these adolescents to take part in close-quarters team-building exercises such as the circle sit or fitting into a map of Israel. And it was at first hard for them to understand how to play their assigned roles well. But as they learned to do so, their confidence increased and so did their vulnerability. I still remember one eighteen-year-old boy, in the post-workshop debriefing, who told all the students and me how, when he was younger, he had lived for over two years in a homeless shelter and had been beaten by his mother's boyfriend. This was a moment of transparency I will never forget, especially when he stated that he wished he had developed these new negotiation skills prior to this beating.

This same case-study approach can be used to engage students in other pressing issues, from environmental issues such as global warming to bullying in US schools, and beyond. The development of such case-study materials comes from my Boston University Educating Global Citizens course. In this semester-long course, limited to fifteen graduate and undergraduate students, I teach the art of negotiation and "getting to yes" conflict management and prevention strategies, and have them take part in a role-play experience using the "Whose Jerusalem?" case study. Then, in teams of three, they propose and develop new geopolitical conflict-resolution case studies as their final projects. And what does this accomplish? This gives me new case studies each year! They may be translated into other languages—Spanish, French, Mandarin, and Arabic, for example—so students can practice the art of negotiation in other languages and learn to compromise and communicate as well.

The one constant of the case-study approach has been outcome: participants enter curious and, by the end, leave more capable and self-confident in their roles as active participants in global dialogue. I don't want to downplay the importance of academic traditions and structure, such as English, mathematics, modern or classical languages, the social sciences, the physical sciences, or the arts. But the rapidly changing times and our increasingly interdependent world have created a new world order that demands unprecedented international engagement and global competency. It's that simple. We need to look honestly at whether, in the interests of tradition, order, and compliance, educational structure has created intellectual prisons, walls that our young people will have to overcome in order to contribute more effectively to the global community. Challenging as it may be to change long-standing habits of education, there is no going back, and no holding back.

CHAPTER SEVEN

Taking the Case Study Global

Education is one thing; responsible, committed, long-term action is another. In part I of this book, I reflected on how global intelligence can teach children about their world in the comfort of their own classrooms and in the forms of various fluencies or literacy: foreign language, technology, media literacy, and more. In part II, I have discussed the action steps that enable more globally intelligent students to become active, powerful, responsible participants in their shrinking world. When we teach children the skills of conflict management and preventive diplomacy through the hands-on, action-packed case-study curriculum, we are creating the mechanism by which students of any age can transform knowledge into action beginning right in the comfort of their own classrooms.

As I mentioned earlier, I've called this the intellectual Outward Bound approach to conflict resolution, because the incredible organization, Outward Bound, focuses on "personal growth through experience and challenge." It revolutionized outdoor education when it reconceptualized traditional camping, offering physically and emotionally challenging exercises along with team building, something that can be an ultimately transformational experience for young people.

My case-study curriculum creates an equally adventuresome, challenging approach to learning, and makes this experience more global in focus, too. It creates challenges for students that far surpass the traditional memorization-and-regurgitation pedagogical approach. It invites students to collaborate and to live, breathe, and absorb new, creative ideas about the world's problems and learn how to deal effectively with them, as teams.

The case-study curriculum can flourish on every level: locally to issues such as date rape and bullying; intrastate to the debates on environmental degradation or alternative sources of power, such as the proposed 130-turbine Cape Cod wind project; nationally to the argument over illegal immigration; and internationally to the Israeli-Palestinian conflict, or the postgenocide Rwandan reconciliation and reconstruction effort. Regrettably, there is no shortage of conflict in our world. Terrorism, genocide, starvation, armed conflicts, trade wars, and environmental disasters scream from the headlines every day. Just think about our Arab Spring—and Arab Fall. The challenge is how to engage millions of American middle and high school students, who are largely disengaged and isolated from world events and devoting their intellectual energies to the traditional study of English, mathematics, the sciences, and US history. However rigorous this course of study, the United States will fail to produce effective globally competent citizens and leaders with a deep understanding of other cultures—and vital conflict management and prevention skills—if schools continue on this largely monolingual, monocultural, standardized exam-driven treadmill that typifies the curriculum in most US public, private, and parochial schools.

Of course, we want our students and our children to succeed. But even more deeply we want our children to live in a world in which a stable, sustainable, peaceful model of coexistence is the universal condition, not a circumstance available only to the privileged few. But how are we acting on these good intentions? How do we translate that desire from an abstract idea (and some would say a fantasy) to an academic reality, in terms of what we teach and how we teach it in K–12 schools? The answer resides at least in part in the case-study curriculum and its increased use in globalizing educational efforts.

Bringing There, Here: Technology and the Case-Study Approach

In the case-study curriculum, a number of the ideas discussed here come together, including proficiency in foreign language when students negotiate in a target language, the eye-opening awareness occasioned by media literacy, the incredibly rich rewards of travel to a place they have studied through role-play simulation, and the profound opportunities available through current technology such as Skyping peers in the areas they are studying.

One example of technology in the service of globalization comes from the "Whose Jerusalem?" case study, during which I often introduce a forty-five-minute e-mail chat or live videoconference session between soon-to-be role-playing students in the United States and their Palestinian and Israeli peers in towns or cities in Israel and the occupied Gaza Strip and West Bank. These peers, from halfway around the world, have volunteered to take part in this exercise as "Seeds"; they have been to the Seeds of Peace International Camp in Maine. The camp, as I mentioned earlier, is an internationally recognized, coexistence, youth leadership program that brings together teens from Israel, Palestine, and other countries with a history of conflict, for serveral three-week sessions each summer. Adolescents from the United States, like Josh, mentioned earlier, are also invited to participate in this program, and some of the past participating students are now camp counselors there. During our e-mail chat or videoconference, some of the "foreign correspondents" are at home, and others are in their high school or university computer labs or dormitory rooms. The US students gather in a conference room, where the live group dialogues appear on a large screen so that all students and teachers can see the online conversations. The students e-mail topics to Palestinian and Israeli students a week before the online communication begins, giving those in the Middle East time to prepare their responses.

Some sample questions include

- What according to you are the main religious, political, and cultural causes of the Palestinian-Israeli conflict?
- When you were younger, how did you respond to conflict in your particular city, town, settlement, or refugee camp?
- How are your responses now different from how they were at that time?
- What role should we as Americans play to assist you in achieving lasting peace between Palestinians and Israelis?

The conversations that ensue are often lively, with the characteristic candor of youth. Students learn about how Palestinian boys and girls their own ages or younger—often age eleven or twelve—are recruited actively by Hamas, Islamic Jihad, or Al Aqsa Martyrs Brigade to become "loyalists," or "cubs," or "flowers" (suicide bombers). They learn that Hamas and Fatah are two thriving Palestinian political parties that have chosen to support change in the Gaza Strip—where Hamas is the party in power—and parts of the West Bank by more peaceful means than intifada. US students also learn about the meaning of "diaspora," the settling of scattered communities of Jews outside Palestine beginning in the sixth century BC when they were exiled to Babylonia and continuing through the twentieth century and the Holocaust to the founding of Israel as a homeland in 1948. And they learn why some Jews moved to the West Bank, established Israeli settlements there, and to this day are determined to stay, hence their need for a fortified West Bank wall to protect themselves against potential suicide bombers and other acts of terror.

Slowly, the American, Palestinian, and Israeli students participating in the e-mail chat, videoconference, or Skype warm to the conversation and take part in respectful and candid dialogues that touch upon some of the major issues in this troubled region. (These are the same issues that the American students grapple with when they wear the hats of Middle East peace negotiators in the live negotiation segment of the case-study role-play.) At times, the students' questions and responses are fascinating, as they try to make sense of the Middle East quagmire:

> *Saeed**, a Palestinian boy from East Jerusalem*: Why don't Israelis understand that they will never, *never*, achieve peace without the creation of a Palestinian state? A political solution has to be reached. Without statehood and basic rights, many Palestinians will continue to support terrorism.

---

* These names have been changed to protect students' privacy.

Khadijah, a Palestinian girl from Hebron: And if the Palestinians had a state, terrorism under Hamas, Al Aqsa, and Islamic Jihad would no longer have the popular support it has now—as a form of "freedom fighters."

Rachel, an Israeli girl from Tel Aviv: But would you want them to think that they won these rights because of terrorist actions, and that perhaps with a little more terrorism, they would be able to take over all of Israel?

Akim, an Israeli boy from West Jerusalem: Netanyahu has repeatedly said that he will continue to oversee Israeli settlement expansion in East Jerusalem while he's in power, but to freeze settlement expansion is a key part of any peace agreement with the Palestinians. In my opinion, with Netanyahu in power, there will not be peace.

Hadassa, an Israeli girl from Tel Aviv: I don't believe peace can be achieved with Mahmoud Abbas in power either, even though he is depicted as a peace maker, he must not anger Palestinian extremists.

Azzan, an Israeli boy from Haifa: And if Abbas is killed or removed from office by Israelis, the Palestinians and others in the Arab world will rise up against Israel, and the situation will only get worse. The real solution lies in compromise. Both sides must give in a little.

Hadiyah, a Palestinian girl from Deirammar, a West Bank refugee camp: Your Secretary of State, HR Clinton, should remind both sides that constant dialogue must take place in order for peace to be achieved, too. Both sides must give up something for any real solution to emerge during this constant dialogue, too.

After interacting with Palestinian and Israeli students via videoconference, one US student commented, "I knew more about the Palestinian side when we started, but after learning more about the security interests of the Netanyahu government in the videoconference session, I became more sympathetic to that side."

Another student's remarks will be interesting to parents and teachers. He said he was impressed that "many Israelis and Palestinians are very well informed on American positions and issues. They are very interested in our political climate, have strong, well-thought-out opinions, and are ready to defend them. We don't have one-tenth the knowledge about their situation, or the world situation in general, for that matter."

Such a live chat, thanks to the power of technology, connects students and often succeeds in generating a lively, respectful international dialogue among these diverse students, planting the seeds of continued communication between US students and their Palestinian and Israeli peers. The American students gain a more profound understanding—from insiders who are also their peers—of Israelis' and Palestinians' cultures, religions, and everyday lives in the center of an often deadly conflict.

In addition to communication with peers halfway around the world, who help the US students to formulate their positions for role-play exercises, students can also participate in interactive lectures on the Middle East conflict by experts from local colleges and universities, if such resources are available, or via videoconferencing or Skype, if they are not. These experts, who may be surprisingly accessible and only awaiting an invitation, can discuss Middle East conflict analysis, negotiation techniques and step-by-step processes of conflict resolution, and the steps necessary for all parties in the Middle East dispute to achieve their goals without compromising the interests of their constituents or leading to possible political or physical assassination. With experts present (for me, these include *Getting to Yes* coauthor Roger Fisher or Mideast experts Denis Sullivan and Anthony Wanis-St. John) or speaking to them via Skype, students can ask questions they have formulated from their reading assignments and their live correspondence with Palestinian and Israeli youths. The poised, interested students can also ask how these peers and experts can play their roles well at the negotiating tables later that same day.

Bringing Here, There: Putting a Case Study to the Test

In many places worldwide, both in the United States and abroad, school-aged children have witnessed their entire communities and cultures devastated by violence. These children may themselves become well-armed killers or child soldiers trained by their mentors to do their bidding as future gang members or young militia. Whatever a student's proximity to violence, he or she may feel called to peace—or called to a "piece of the action" of bloodshed and vengeance. What tools should we give to US youth, future peacemakers who are or will be called to mediate and those called to violence so that they might think before acting in cruel, often deadly ways? This is where preventive diplomacy can make the biggest difference. One example of this was not here in the United States, but rather half a world away.

When I traveled to Rwanda for the first time in July 2005, I was a teacher and the founder and executive director of Axis of Hope. I spent two-and-a-half weeks in the capital city of Kigali, working with Rwandan adolescents—thirty students and eight teachers from two schools—on conflict management and prevention skills as part of the national government's reconciliation initiative following the height of the country's 1994 genocide. But I was worried; at the time I only had one preventive diplomacy role-play case study, "Whose Jerusalem?" and I would be working with students who lived in Rwanda, far from the Middle East. Roughly two-thirds of the students were from Green Hills Academy, a private school attended by all of President Paul Kagame's four children, as well as children of other influential parents—Partners in Health cofounder Dr. Paul Farmer's children, for example—who were successful Rwandan business or medical or community leaders, or members of families from other countries living and working in Rwanda. The other third were students from the FAWE School, a girls' school opened originally for post-genocide orphan girls, many of whom had lost their entire families in the genocide. These were all girls, as the Hutu extremists, or Hutu Power, had focused on killing adults and boys first, eliminating those considered the smart, strong, healthy core of the Tutsi and moderate Hutu people. They spared many of the girls for rape, assuming they would die anyway from complications of HIV (since many of the rapists were HIV positive, this was called "the slow bullet"), physical abuse, or starvation. Now, eleven years later, the school's students included not only orphans but also girls whose families had returned from the Rwanda diaspora, which had begun in 1959. You could say that all of them, regardless of ethnic background, were in some way survivors of a horrible shared history but also that they were adolescents: smart, resilient, sturdy, and clearly the next generation of Rwanda's leadership. These are the major questions: President Kagame's unification efforts notwithstanding, would these young people feel called to the work of peace, or would they be forced to return to conflict? What would they be taught, and how? How would they be prepared with the skills they would need to manage inevitable ethnic tension in the future and build a culture of peaceful coexistence on ground that still held so many of the remains of the brutal past?

In answering these questions, I often think about those tragic hundred days in 1994, when, from the town of Gisenyi in the west on the shores of Lake Kivu to the capital of Kigali in the center and to Kibungo in the east, Hutu Power soldiers and Interahamwe militia (radical armed youth who were Hutu Power military point guards) carried rifles, machetes, and nail-studded "porcupine clubs." They also carried the addresses of those to be killed: Tutsis and moderate Hutus who had married Tutsis or had taken them in to their homes to protect them.

Former president Bill Clinton, perhaps feeling guilty for not intervening to prevent the one hundred days of genocide, stated in an address that appears in the introduction to the film *Sometimes in April*:

> Innocent people gathered in any place they felt safe from the Hutu Power killing squads. By the thousands, they sought refuge in churches, hospitals, schools, tiny bathrooms, wells, and irrigation ditches. And by the thousands, when they were found, they were slaughtered by the Hutu Power soldiers. The old and the young, the men and the women, the healthy and the ill, all killed;

> killed because their identity cards said they were Tutsi, or because they had a Tutsi parent or because someone thought they looked like a Tutsi. Or they were slain as Hutu moderates because they protected Tutsis, or because they would not countenance a policy that sought to wipe out people who just the day before or for years before had been their friends and neighbors.

When I first arrived in Kigali, in the summer of 2005, I asked myself how I was going to teach preventive diplomacy to this first generation of survivors of the genocide—an atrocity barely a decade prior to my arrival, something in the aftermath that is still simmering across the country like an active volcano? After all, preventive diplomacy and conflict management and prevention were anything but "academic" to these students and teachers. Their country had been rebuilding quite rapidly since 1994, but the fear that former Hutu radicals might attempt to retake center stage was and is ever present. They have tried several times since 1994. To this day, many former Hutu Power members are living near Goma, Democratic Republic of Congo, near the border with Rwanda. They have changed their party name to FDLR, are well financed, and are well armed by certain foreign governments and sympathizers still living and working in Rwanda or in the international community. There is also a genuine fear of "insider Tutsis," those former Tutsis who remained within the borders of Rwanda at the height of the genocide in 1994, who survived, and who do not agree that President Kagame and other former Tutsis—who grew up outside Rwanda—should now be in power.

President Kagame is bent on reconciliation and reconstruction of his country. A former Tutsi and RPF leader who grew up in a refugee camp in southern Uganda, he has declared tribal or ethnic identifications to be invalid and made it public policy to refer to citizens only as Rwandans. President Kagame and Ambassador Richard Sezibera, former Rwandan ambassador to the United States, then ambassador to the Great Lakes Region, and now secretary general of the East African Community, believe in teaching youth in Rwanda to become leaders who will prevent future conflicts, especially genocide. This is why I went there to work with the students and teachers in 2005.

Kagame was attempting to integrate the values, ethics, and character of peaceful coexistence into every aspect of Rwandan life, so essential to the positive transformation of peoples, now and in the future. Preventive diplomacy training for youth would offer a way to deepen Rwandan students' understanding of the cultural, social, and psychological tools required for coexistence, and provide an opportunity for experiential learning in which they could practice their skills in the safe space of an educational environment—take risks, make mistakes, and live to tell about it.

How could I teach them these skills? To be honest, I was nervous because before my first trip to Rwanda, I only had one case study that I could use with youth there. But, as I came to discover, focusing on another conflict that existed thousands of miles from Rwanda was the perfect way to begin to teach these youth conflict management and prevention skills. In 2005, because the "Whose Jerusalem?" case study was the only one I had, I decided to teach the Rwandan students these conflict management and prevention skills by transporting them intellectually to a different landscape of conflict, far away from the familiar territory of Rwanda.

For five days, from 8:30 a.m. to 2:30 p.m., these Rwandan teenaged boys and girls became Israelis and Palestinians and members of the Arab League and the Quartet. Each morning began with Outward Bound icebreaker and team-building exercises. As the exercises unfolded, the students hesitated only briefly, then intuitively responded as collaborators (excited conspirators) to control the exercises, leading and following one another to the finish. As they warmed up to the tasks and the freedom to take the initiative in problem solving, I watched the rather conservative faculty members from both schools eyeing the scene a little nervously; they weren't accustomed to such bold spontaneity and freedom of physical movement and verbal expression by their students. Their faces were serious, often somber. On a few faces I saw raised eyebrows that could best be translated as "What in the heck is this?!" In many schools in many countries in which I've worked with youth, I find some teachers who are open to the experience of students leading the learning activites, and many others who are much less amenable and much more skeptical.

The seminar included the same assigned readings on the Middle East conflict I had used with youth in the United States and a time line of the conflict; brief lectures on the political, religious, historical, economic, social, and geographic facets of the conflict; role-play exercises with students representing different stakeholders on all sides of the conflict; and, in the end—and this is extremely important—how they could relate their ideas of negotiations leading to more peaceful coexistence in the Middle East to the current Rwandan efforts to achieve unity, reconciliation, and reconstruction in a peaceful manner.

In amazing serendipity, the mental change of venue freed these Rwandan students from the constraints imposed by their roots in their home soil of conflict, and brought out their natural intellectual energy and curiosity about a conflict in another part of our increasingly interdependent world. Like their peers in the United States, they were excited by a meaningful global challenge, by intelligent "agree to disagree" debate, and by conflict management and prevention skill-building exercises.

Since the Kigali, Rwanda, student group included visiting students from the FAWE school, many whom the Green Hills Academy students had never met, the preliminary icebreaker and team-building exercises were especially important for the students to get to know and relate to one another. Their schools had no history of shared activity, and the students came from starkly different socioeconomic backgrounds. They proved to have two things in common, however. First, all were accustomed to the culture of order and obedience, in which adults were the dispensers of education and children were the receivers. Second, once they felt free to turn that system upside down, to take charge, and to engage fully and without restraint, the Rwandan students showed the same energy and enthusiasm—something I now believe is universal among young people—for listening, learning, leading, pushing themselves hard, taking intellectual risks, and wanting to learn more.

As the week progressed, the students got the hang of the case-study preparation and role-play activity, becoming more at ease with the freedom to work together without receiving prompts or demands from teachers. They became more engaged with each other, and primed for the upcoming conflict management exercise too. The activity was presented in English, and of course those who were conversant in English stepped into natural leadership roles, more confident than those who relied on others to translate from French or Kinyarwanda to English, much as monolingual Americans often have to do in similar circumstances. But even those who did not understand or speak English well began to gain confidence, as they would at times communicate in short Kinyarwanda sentences or—as students often do—use the power of body language to ask a question or get an answer.

I had wondered whether the students, in a culture eleven years beyond the height of genocide in 1994 and with the possibility of the genocide regime's return, would take actively to the Middle East conflict presented in "Whose Jerusalem?" The faraway conflict, though not their own, turned out to be a perfect vehicle for them to discuss important conflict-resolution themes, and to debate issues that have plagued not only the Middle East, but Rwanda as well. They eagerly assumed the identities of their role-play characters, clearly understanding the deep historical division between sides in the Middle East and the passions each side brings to negotiations. They practiced and refined their new skills as they worked through the scripted and unscripted conflict-resolution role-play exercises, too.

In one heated moment, the daughter of Rwanda's former ambassador to the United States and the oldest son of Rwanda's president—whose families are very close friends—found themselves yelling at each other, each one absorbed in his and her respective (and adversarial) roles. The outspoken and verbally assertive behavior of the very bright girl—completely in character for the role-play activity but uncommon in the Rwandan culture—astonished her classmates. For a shining moment, it was clear that they were both unsure whether it was all right for this to be happening, but it was interesting to see both continue to argue passionately, while several other students, including the president's daughter, quickly moved forward to defuse the tension. At the end of the five-day workshop, the student recommendations for the division of Jerusalem were included in a typed and signed position paper on Green Hills Academy stationery. Copies of the recommendation were then sent directly to Rwanda's president Paul Kagame, as well as then-US president George W. Bush and then-US secretary of state Condoleezza Rice.

The week of this preventive diplomacy role-play exercise using the "Whose Jerusalem?" case study proved a success in many ways. Students raved about the experience. Even teachers who had been reluctant at first to cede control of the class activity to students became more comfortable with the lively activity and debate when they saw how passionate—and responsible—their students could be. As for the students, they seemed to bloom in the unaccustomed attention and intellectual interaction with each other, with me, and with their teachers. The smallest gestures had such an impact; they were thrilled when I taught them the high-five palm slap and the combination handshake/quick hug so common among teens (boys, anyway) in the United States. None of them—not the orphans or the affluent children—had experienced this kind of cheerful, positive interaction from teachers in the school setting. It was clear to me that they were hungry for positive adult attention and interaction in a world where adults were completely immersed in rebuilding a nation and, understandably, in controlling circumstances to ensure an orderly reconstruction process in their society. Order and compliance is one way to keep the peace. But when adult guidance becomes adult control, it can also take a toll on the intellectual development and peaceful leadership potential of the rising generation.

What did I learn during this extraordinary week with Rwandan adolescents in the summer of 2005? It is possible to teach youth in the US and in Rwanda this different, deeper way of viewing the world, understanding it, interacting, and preventing conflicts more effectively. They can and should learn the conflict-resolution skills that lead to preventive steps and solutions, rather than preemptive strikes, as the US invasion of Iraq was labeled in order to justify it. As I have learned in my years of teaching, children are quick to adapt to a variety of educational settings and approaches, and to adopt what I call a universal code of compassion—a willingness to accept others and respond to them with respect, appreciation, and the intention to understand the reality of their lives: their cultures, religions, and social and economic conditions; their relationships with each other and the wider world. We have only to tap into this incredibly deep wellspring of potential for peacemaking and peace maintenance—coexistence—and provide a channel for it to flow to critical fields of endeavor in school, at home, and abroad, during the formative years of our nation's and the world's youth.

This can and does work right in the United States as well. As I mentioned in the previous chapter, the "Whose Jerusalem?" case study was used effectively in a Chicago inner-city public high school, where many students attending were members of Chicago gangs. Every participant had previous behavior issues and had been disciplined by the school, so the workshop was also a means to stimulate constructive behavior. These students instinctively knew the face of violence and had witnessed its repercussions. The tension between African Americans and Latinos in their neighborhoods could and did easily result in fatalities. The lessons they learned in only two days—communication, compromise, compassion—could and did lead to a better understanding of how to prevent these often deadly problems.

Because the case study appears to deal with issues that are "out there" at first, it gets students in any school setting, public, private, or parochial, to understand conflict on a broad scale and encourages collaboration in creative ways, including the especially important development of negotiation skills. It also knocks down social barriers, as students rally together rather than against each other to solve complex problems. Some students even report that epiphany of critical thought, the "aha" moment about being global citizens actively engaged in conflict management and prevention elsewhere in the world. After participating in the "Whose Jerusalem?" case study, one Rwandan student said, "Mr. Carl, the past five days here have taught me much more than I thought I knew. Thanks to you, Mr. Carl, I have developed a sense of reconciliation, coexistence with my fellow people, and much more." And one African American gang member said, "My eyes have been opened up to what's going on in the world and how we should work out our disagreements in a more peaceful way, by talking it out, rather than through violence."

That is the point: teaching students to become true team players in the practice of conflict management and prevention. Whether students are addressing hypothetical violence halfway around the world or actual violence in their own backyards, the workshops teach them the importance of understanding, learning to listen, compassion, and so much more.

CHAPTER EIGHT

Service Learning

The Power of Experiential Education

Students need to be resilient thinkers, whether they are in the classroom or on the sports field or out in the real world of diverse obstacles and circumstances. But they don't get that way by learning to study, memorize, and regurgitate information we force them to master or by preparing for standardized exams, such as the SAT, SAT II, or AP. A sound knowledge base is necessary, but decades of research tells us that a well-thought-out mixture of hands-on, multisensory experiences, coupled with time to reflect and absorb these experiences, is the process through which young minds may more effectively learn and then integrate what they know, what they think and feel, and how they can act on it into their daily lives.

I call this a form of experiential education, and, as I have tried to demonstrate, this begins right in your own classroom through role-play simulation exercises based on case studies. This experiential education process can be deepened through community service, or service learning, as John Dewey called it. Dewey challenged educators from the 1910s to the 1930s to develop educational programs that would not be isolated from real-life experience. "The inclination to learn from life itself and to make the conditions of life such that all will learn in the process of living is the finest product of schooling," he advocated in his 1916 book *Democracy and Education*. Dewey believed that "students should be involved in real-life tasks and challenges: Maths could be learnt via learning proportions in cooking or figuring out how long it would take to get from one place to another by mule. History could be learned by experiencing how people lived, geography, what the climate was like, and how plants and animals grew."

Dewey's philosophy still lies at the heart of many bold educational experiments, such as Outward Bound and mine at Axis of Hope.

Experiential learning affects us in profound ways, too. Even the briefest moments in life are the building blocks of emotional experience and memory, says Harvey L. Rich, MD, founder of the American Psychoanalytic Foundation and consultant to the World Bank on postconflict recovery in cultures traumatized by war and violence. In his book *In the Moment: Embracing the Fullness of Life*, Rich describes how every moment "contains content"—that is, action, thought, or feeling, sometimes all three. When we learn, if a lesson is to be truly imprinted on us and not simply memorized, we must in some way receive that content or, in other words, experience what we are learning. Experience imposes itself on all the levels of the brain and central nervous system, from the spinal cord to the brain stem—the reptilian midbrain where the viscera is learning that which we are experiencing—to the thalamic brain, where affect is attached to what we are learning, to the higher cerebral hemispheres where cognitive awareness and, most importantly, synthesis take place. (When we memorize a lesson, it is almost completely done in those top cerebral hemispheres, and the real depth of learning does not, unfortunately, take place.)

This is how experiential education, in the context of in-class conflict-resolution role-play simulations or service-learning exercises, "imposes itself"; it virtually changes the brain and shapes a child's mind for increased social consciousness and global responsibility at any age, whatever the mix of developmental factors they bring to the moment. A parent or a teacher may give a heartfelt lecture on the importance of contributing or giving back in the form of community service, and the young person may hear and duly note that lecture, but neurologically and cognitively it may be traveling that well-worn path of most adult lectures (whether they are delivered in the classroom or at the dining table at home), to the part of the brain where "OMG, not another spelling list . . . ," "Oh no, not more US history facts I have to memorize . . . ," and "Ah yes, the promise I made to clean up my room and finish my homework . . . haahaa!" are stored. However, add free pizza, the names of a few good friends, the promise of interaction online or face-to-face with the other students, or an out-of-school adventure, and the neurotransmitters literally jump the track, zinging rapidly through the parts of the brain that light up with sensory stimulation and generate excitement like a lit-up pinball machine.

Whatever the initial trigger that gets students moving—pizza, pals, or even academic extra credit—once they are engaged in the shared experience of partnering in meaningful work, it is the continuing social-emotional-intellectual charge of that experience that grabs their attention and keeps them revved up for learning. The community-service experience of feeling competent and useful in helping others, with rigorous study before, well-prepared field work during, and carefully orchestrated debriefing activities after, makes service learning a rich, often transformative (educational) lesson.

What specifically makes service learning so relevant, even critical, to success in teaching global competence and citizenship? One explanation lies in the understanding that, unlike the mass of facts and commentary that comprises our knowledge about a subject such as US history, mathematics, or English (all essential components of a strong global education), global intelligence represents a relationship—a connection between the facts learned in the classroom and the meaning we assign them, and how we are moved to act upon these ideas, too. It is the difference between asking, "Where is my brother?" and asking, "Am I my brother's savior?" It is the difference between asking, "What are the projects so-called 'do-gooders' are supporting?" and asking, "Where are the projects our teachers are setting up for us, and what are people living there experiencing?" The first question asks for information; the other, for a moral point of view. Global competence, literacy, and responsibility assume a point of view; a relationship based on not only thinking about, but understanding and caring about others. It is an expression of the way in which we experience ourselves in relationship to the larger world and the circumstances that affect others in that global community. So, while our relationship with the larger world is informed by our knowledge and understanding (or by our ignorance) of it, a sense of global responsibility especially comes from a deeper, more psychologically complex and powerful place.

If we want to instill in our youth a sense of global competence, literacy, and responsibility, and if we want to teach these skills well in schools, then we have to take students out of the educational containers of parent, school board, or faculty predetermined curricula and into the real world, more effectively and now. We need to move beyond school-based diversity workshops and service-learning planning sessions to quality interaction with local communities where people live and struggle and celebrate the meaning of everyday life. When we take students beyond the comfortable cocoon of school (and home) and provide them with opportunities to not just discuss but to meet, interact with, and help others, we can teach them not only to appreciate the situations, strengths, and vulnerability of those they are helping, but to reflect on themselves and their roles in helping others. We can teach them to reflect on themselves, their friends and families, and their roles in this shrinking world. When, in the context of these unfamiliar and perhaps challenging circumstances, students learn to interact in new and creative ways with their teachers and parents, with peers, and with other people in local areas, they learn more about classmates and siblings, themselves, and the collective spirit that emerges in tackling a challenge together, as a team.

Local Service Learning: In Your Own Backyard

I remember hearing the term "think globally, act locally" on the radio on my way to work one morning when it first came into vogue. Around the same time, I read about the idea of raising youth to accomplish goals that are *glocal* in nature, fusing together the words global and local. They both seemed like very simple but powerful ideas. As I pondered these terms, I knew how important it was—and is—to teach youth to focus upon what is happening in our ever-changing world. But I also realized that it was and is important to constantly think about the cultivation of one's own garden as Voltaire taught us in the classic *Candide*—and by this, I mean the local community—especially because not all students can afford to travel overseas in order to experience service learning.

I will never forget one excellent example of this. One year, during a "middle school community-service day," eight of my ninth-grade advisees hosted a group of sixteen children, aged seven to ten, from the Italian Home for Children in Jamaica Plain, a wonderful historic neighborhood in Boston. The school is a place dear to my heart, a day school and boarding facility for underprivileged children who study and/or live there because of often tragic—or, as the state of Massachusetts calls them—"negative" home lives, including physical and emotional abuse. On a chilly but sunny January day, sixteen children came to our school's state-of-the-art athletic center where, as soon as they arrived, I felt my heart racing. I asked myself: "Are we going to be able to work with these kids? Their age group is not what I'm used to. Will they actually have fun in this middle and upper school athletic environment?" At that point in my career, I was teaching seventh- and eighth-grade boys who wore coats and ties to their prominent Boston-area all-boys' school each day. I worried about whether my advisees and I would be able to interact correctly with these visiting children on new turf for them. What happened next showed me just how quickly youth can transform themselves into "cultural chameleons." I watched my eight advisees greet all of the visiting students and teachers as they arrived in the parking lot and then lead them into the school's athletic center. I remember watching one of my students teaching children like Jada, a ten-year-old girl, how to play a creative game of one-on-one handball on the squash courts with a tennis ball, hitting the ball against the far wall with the palms of their hands, or teaching Luke, a nine year old, to play Wiffle ball in one of the two gymnasiums. After a morning of fun playing games in the squash courts and the gym, we took our bag lunches, nicely prepared by my school's kitchen staff, upstairs. There, we talked about where we were raised, about what we were learning or teaching in school, and about the wonderful things and also the problems in our lives.

After lunch, I had my advisees, several of whom were talented basketball players, come to the gym with their new friends. There, they hit the court before their own more formal varsity basketball practice later that afternoon, to play hoops with all of the kids from the Jamaica Plain school. I sat with the teachers and trip chaperones in the bleachers, watching the children and my advisees laugh, while my boys passed the ball to the young kids and taught them moves on the court. I felt I was being taught something as well. Even though as teachers we are supposed to have all the answers, I clearly didn't when this day began. And now what I saw was extraordinary: these talented student athletes were able to relate to the younger children. They invented spontaneous games that kept the children laughing. Several got down on their knees to be closer in height to the visiting children. Other boys allowed the younger children to ride on their backs to be taller and to be able to get the ball in the basket more easily. I realized, sitting there in the stands that afternoon, that I could rely on students, who often surpass us in intuitive heart, to not only help younger, disadvantaged children like these. They could also pick me up emotionally. Even though my students did not know any of these children, they became like their big brothers immediately, and they became in many ways like my sons. They might not have known it then, but I was incredibly proud of them.

As we said goodbye to the visiting children and teachers in the parking lot that afternoon, the children thanked us and, looking their new older brothers and me straight in the eye, they asked, "Can we come back sometime soon?" Can you imagine what you see in a nine-year-old girl's brown eyes when she asks this question? Innocence, a search for hope, and an eagerness for a better life. After the children left, I had a debriefing session with the students who had been helping out all day, prior to their afternoon basketball, hockey, or squash practices. In our discussion, they shared how much they had experienced that day, and how different it had been from what they expected. Each student asked if he could go to the school in Jamaica Plain to visit the children and to work and play with them again soon. And as we departed that afternoon, after a fun day of working with the children and their teachers, I reminded my students and advisees of the words of Martin Luther King Jr. on service: "An individual has not started living until he can rise above the narrow confines of his individualistic concerns to the broader concerns of all humanity."

Many of the boys took that day's lesson and Martin Luther King's quote to heart, as they proposed and were approved to take part in a spring project that year, working with these same children for one day in their own elementary school. One of those boys even returned there to work four days per week as a senior project during his last semester at our school. He chose to remain engaged, right up to his last day of high school. It had all started with that original service-learning exercise involving our school and those children from Jamaica Plain.

National Service Learning: Selma, a Bridge to History

I often think about the daily four-mile run I would take through the woods in Belmont, Massachusetts. Every day, I would stop beside a pond and throw a small rock into the middle of it. When I did so, I thought, "A stone thrown into the middle of a perfectly still pond has a ripple effect of creating circular waves." So, too, do powerful service-learning exercises that begin locally. The middle school community-service day I just described, which enables small groups of students and teachers to serve others in the local area, can construct an excellent foundation of giving back to others in other ways. And this includes regional or national service learning trips involving students, teachers, and parents, if they too can come along. I recall one ten-day service-learning journey from Boston to Selma, Alabama, the geographic heart of the 1960s US civil rights struggle, offered by a friend and former colleague at this school. The students on this trip traveled by bus, slept on the floor of a church, and together with their teachers and chaperones cooked their own food or were the guests of local organizations found through networking with the Black Belt Community Foundation and the Central Alabama Housing Authority. As the chief planner of this and subsequent trips to the area, friend and former colleague Donna David says, "We always eat well when we go down South." This demonstrates, with all of the fluencies and action steps in this book, there are both more immediate and more adventurous possibilities available that are not too expensive to plan and execute. In other words, one mustn't confuse adventurous with expensive.

In March 1965, the violence of segregation met the courage of nonviolent protest, led by Dr. Martin Luther King Jr., and the activists' ultimate victory in Selma galvanized national attention and support for the Voting Rights Act. In recent years, the growing body of literature (including history texts and commentary, documentaries, and other visual and audio materials, and highly evolved study guides about this transformational period in US history) has provided a cornucopia of resources for students and teachers. But Donna, the school health director who was and still is also the school's community-service coordinator, wanted to not only teach students about King and his experience in Selma, but to let students see, smell, live, and breathe Selma as it exists today, years after King's personal journey there. How was she going to do so?

It began with Donna's passionate sales pitch at a "meet and greet" events. Despite a packed day of classes, interested students were invited to bring a brown-bag lunch to a discussion session with the person who would become their faculty trip leader to learn more about the trip. Then, for six weeks before their departure, Donna and her soon-to-be Selma-bound students studied portions of the award-winning PBS television documentary series *Eyes on the Prize.* The fourteen-hour series uses contemporary interviews and historic footage to cover the key events of the civil rights movement from 1954 to 1985. Donna's students focused on the Selma story and the historic march by King and others across the Edmund Pettus Bridge near a church they planned to visit. They studied the economic and political climate of the area. On blogs and online journals, they learned about past and present local residents' lives and their work in Selma.

They'd done their homework and felt well prepared as they boarded the bus from Boston to the Ebenezer Baptist Church in Selma, where they would stay during their visit. Along the way, the students watched the landscape change from the flavor of New England to that of south of the Mason-Dixon line, so when they got off the bus at the church, they felt slightly more acclimated to the South. Yet, as Donna says, "nothing prepared us for the personal stories of the people there, or for the genuineness and friendliness that seemed to be everyone's way of life."

Church members had prepared dinner for the students before they arrived. And students ate gratefully and listened mesmerized to the stories of several local residents who had lived through those times and been active in the protests and the march King led across the Pettus Bridge, just a short distance from the church. The students were aware of the church's special connection to those historic events; the Reverend Dr. Frederick D. Reese, then pastor of the church and president of the county Voter's League, had been a local leader in the civil rights and voting rights march and movement. He and his family had been personally targeted for violence; his home had been firebombed by segregationists during that period. Reese had been a friend and colleague of King and, as an outspoken community leader himself, he had walked alongside King on the Selma bridge on that historic day.

Students saw the historical period and that day in Selma come alive in the hosts' eyes and in their stories of the community's hopes and dreams, as well as the fear, loss, and anger of that time. As they listened to personal recollections of and reflections about the march, learned of clandestine meetings to plan nonviolent protests, and heard stories of routine police harassment and brutality against blacks at the time, a church member interrupted to ask them if they would like to meet the Rev. Dr. Reese, who happened to be in the building for other reasons that evening. They were astonished to find themselves face-to-face with this historic figure, who, now in his seventies, welcomed them to his church, answered questions, and encouraged them. Then he offered to take them for a walk across the famous Pettus Bridge. This work, and this entire experience, will long remain in the minds of the participating students

The rest of the students' work-study stay in this inspiring community centered on helping residents with home painting. Many of the people were living in severe financial hardship, unemployed or working for very low wages, and their homes sorely needed repairs and maintenance. The students' experience of meeting people living in these conditions—in the United States, not some distant third-world country—was a lesson no book or even documentary could have delivered with the same impact.

As Donna recalled:

> It was difficult for our kids to see that one house we were painting had gaping holes in it—the entire back of the house simply had old doors propped up against it to protect the family from rain. Mice and other "things" came and went from these openings. We were told to use pieces of heavy cardboard to close up the openings on the front and the side—we felt badly that we could not do more. In an ideal world, we would have had lumber to do some repairs and then do the painting.

The lesson was not about pity, however, but a much deeper appreciation for the qualities that make us all human and that we all share, from the desire for freedom and respect, to the need to feel a connection to others, to finding a way to contribute and give back to others. Donna continues:

> When we first came to the site, there was an older woman sitting on her front porch, on an old sofa that was up on cinder blocks—she virtually had to be coaxed off her sofa so that we could move it and begin the washing and painting of the house. We moved a chair to the front yard for her to sit in, but she stayed in the house until the afternoon, when she ventured out with a bowl of collard greens she had prepared. I sat with her and she talked a bit. She told me how to make collard greens so I could do it when I got home. (And yes, I did make them once I got home! It reminded me of my grandma who used to make the same thing.) There was also a young boy who lived in this house—a boy of about five or six—and I told our students that it could make a difference to this young boy if they were to ask for his help. I had the students introduce themselves to him, and we gave him painting goggles to wear and a small brush so that he, too, could help paint his own house. I was able to remind my own students that rather than always having "things done for you," it's human nature to

> like to be involved and contribute. I would like to imagine this boy will remember this experience of painting his own house, and that he will know that he, too, can make a difference.

For a study unit that, in so many ways, was about the power of one person to effect change, it was a valuable moment that allowed students to see how many ways, and in how many dimensions, these ideas—John F. Kennedy's "Let us never negotiate out of fear, but let us never fear to negotiate" and "There is inherited wealth in this country and also inherited poverty"—resonate. The trip to Selma held special meaning for some of the students who were African American, too, but for every student—regardless of race or ethnicity—it was a recognition and a realization that this complex story was part of their personal history, of their heritage as US citizens.

Global Service Learning: From Jamaica Plain to the Home of Hope

If you want to understand the power of experiential education for a young person, it helps to remember how deeply they experience so much of life that we adults overlook. When I was nearing the end of my two weeks in Rwanda (detailed in chapter 7), I carefully planned a daylong service-learning trip for the Green Hills Academy and FAWE students with whom I was working, taking them to the Home of Hope orphanage, right in the center of the capital city of Kigali, Rwanda, and just down the hill from Hôtel des Mille Collines, or Hotel Rwanda. And how did I propose this idea to the participating students? On the final Friday of our conflict-resolution exercises, I offered to take along any students who wished to go with me, as a service-learning experience, to the orphanage run by protégés of Mother Teresa, the following Monday. I expected very few takers; despite the orphanage's relatively close proximity to the two schools, none of the students had ever visited it or volunteered in it. I did not think that they would be comfortable going there, even for part of a day. But to my surprise, every student stepped forward and asked to go. Security arrangements were made for our visit, especially because two of President Kagame's children would be going there with the group. And, interestingly, the schools' administrators approved of the visit to the infant and young children's quarters of the orphanage, but asked me that, for security reasons, I not allow the students to visit the elderly. They felt there was no way to know how those genocide survivors would react to the students, many of whom came from families who, because of the diaspora that began in 1959, had grown up in other African or European nations and had now returned to their homeland, or, as many would say, had "reconquered" what was not rightfully their homeland. As a result, there was a genuine concern for the students' safety during the visit.

In the Home of Hope, the Rwandan students literally stepped into a world with which they were unfamiliar. As they walked down the gently sloping concrete steps beside one of the first buildings in which they would be working, they heard the cries of infants echoing out of the screened windows. The students proceeded, in single file, down a dimly lit, long, narrow hallway. They could smell the pungent odor of urine and feces, as if oozing from the walls, and they could hear infants' faint cries echoing from a room on the left and another, the intensive care room, on the right. They also noticed one long, very large bedroom further down the hallway on the left, crowded with rows of light-blue cribs, with five to six infants standing or sitting in each one. There the orphans were staring wide-eyed at the students as they entered the room, seventy or so toddlers waiting expectantly for food and attention. It was standing room only, their tiny fists gripping the sidebars, many faces showing smiles, some showing intense fear. It was not, after all, a happy journey that landed them here as orphans. In this dark room of the orphanage, as I had told the students before we began our work that day, these innocent young orphans were prisoners of poverty, yet the students' attention and feeding would offer them a tiny bit of freedom from poverty, if only for a day.

Our first goal was to serve breakfast to each child: on this and every morning, warm porridge was prepared in a large, covered, metal pot, similar to a huge lobster pot, over an open fire in a roof-covered area just behind the building. I took the group of students and introduced them to the cooks and the breakfast crew of young women who would be helping them feed the children. The crew, themselves orphans now working in the same orphanage where they had grown up, greeted the students in Kinyarwanda. At one end of the outdoor kitchen, hundreds of the small, empty metal bowls and metal baby spoons crowded outgoing trays destined for the room full of cribs and the rows of long tables in the outdoor dining hall, where under a cheap aluminum awning, the three- to five-year-old children waited eagerly on the concrete patio to eat. At the other end of the outdoor kitchen, stacks of empty bowls formed a wobbly skyline of dirty dishes, covered with a haze of flies, toppling at last into a sink of soapy dishwater and the quick hands of the cleanup crew.

When the student volunteers returned to the crib room with two bowls of warm porridge, and two spoons each, the infants and toddlers seated inside the cribs reached through the bars, grasping for something as simple as a spoonful of porridge, a hug, or a touch—almost as developmentally important for this age as nutrition. As I watched the orphans reach through the bars to connect with the Kigali students (one-third of whom were orphans themselves), I thought of the many ways in which schools and even education itself, anywhere in the world, can become their own kinds of prisons or walled enclosures, which keep our youth from connecting with a larger, interdependent world that is vital for them to get to know well. This is not just a world for them to know about, from the comfort of the wide-screen television or the MacBook Pro at home, or in classrooms with the traditional textbooks. This is a world that more students must get to know personally by studying about issues like these, and then being offered hands-on experiences, in their own backyards locally, nationally, or halfway around the world. For the Rwandan students I took to Home of Hope that day, the bars had been lifted, figuratively. This bar-lifting liberty began in the newfound freedom they had experienced in our conflict management and prevention activities, including the icebreaker and team-building exercises, the case-study role-play exercises, and the interaction with me as a conflict-resolution instructor. The bars were then breached in a very real, experiential manner when we left the confines of the school to visit, live, breathe, see, smell, and touch the orphanage on that unforgettable day. The day changed the students' views of how they could continue to work with these children after they returned to their own homes. It also changed my view of how I must educate students in areas of potential conflict, like Rwanda, and also taught me the importance of bringing this belief in experiential service learning to US classrooms as well.

The following fall, I put together a slide show of photos from my summer experience in Rwanda and showed this to 425 students and 50 faculty members during my school's morning meeting in the nondenominational chapel. I titled the presentation "Think about Giving Back." At the end of the fifteen-minute show, which was set to the song "Bad," by my favorite band, U2, I asked all interested upper-school students to come to my classroom during the week to discuss the possibility of going to Rwanda with me the following summer. That same day, four students came to my classroom at different times during the day: Winston, Marcus, Burch, and Jake. All four looked me straight in the eye and said with earnest passion, "May we join your Rwanda team?" I said, "Of course," and we never looked back. That day has led to friendships with these four boys, now young men, who are still like sons to me.

In late June the year after first visiting Rwanda and working with Rwandan students there, I returned to the same Kigali orphanage, Home of Hope. This time I was with those four inspired Boston-area students, who had gone through orientation in my classroom and in the school's faculty meeting room with their parents. They had each applied for and received their passports. They had gotten shots for yellow fever, filled anti-malaria pill prescriptions, and so much more, in preparation for our ten-day trip. The families of the students in Kigali with whom I had worked the year before hosted these American boys too. Each day, the four students and I joined the 270 orphans and elderly residents at Home of Hope for eight hours. Winston and Marcus had just completed their sophomore years of high school, Jake and Burch, their freshmen years, and all were either fourteen or fifteen years old. We were there to work, teach, and learn in this small, peaceful, walled-in enclave operated by Mother

Teresa's Missionaries of Charity. Each day, the four boys donned colorful cotton smocks to feed the porridge to one and two year olds in their cribs, as the Rwandan students had done one year earlier. We all sat on long, low, wooden benches, one bowl on each side of each of us, "double-fist feeding" those wonderful children through the slats of the cribs. We then went outside to the sunny courtyard and, in two rickety classrooms with plywood walls, taught English to five- and six-year-old Rwandan children. We joined these older children for recess in the protected courtyard, riding the seesaw, playing pickup soccer games, or allowing them to crawl all over us, to laugh, to get attention.

Each day, the boys also visited the elderly, within the confines of the orphanage, just down the hill from the orphans' buildings. The old people who reside there, many since the height of the genocide in 1994, had been orphaned due to the loss of their families killed in the violence or the survivors' inability to care for them. Most were very kind, with smiles like crescent moons and wrinkles more magical and indicative of their lives than the classic crow's-feet we so often discuss in the United States. Most of these elderly were ill or incapacitated, many profoundly brutalized by the Hutu Power soldiers some thirteen years before, about the time my students' families were videotaping their toddler sons' first steps. The old people smiled in the warmth of the boys' companionship and taught them simple phrases in Kinyarwanda.

Our experiences at the Kigali orphanage as a small group of Americans will fill our conversations for years to come: the memory of each child cuddled, fed, played, or talked with; the rooms packed wall-to-wall with cribs and beds; the sound of scores of babies and young children crying; and the unnatural silence in rooms full of children who were too sick to cry. But one memory, one moment, stands out most powerfully for me, like Saint-Exupéry's baobab in his classic *Le Petit Prince*.

It was a fleeting moment as the four boys and I traveled between the long, narrow houses in the compound. Walking down a gradually descending staircase to cross a small courtyard for a visit to the elderly residents in the adjacent building, we noticed a sister of the order just outside. She sat on a long, wooden bench in the shade under the slightly extending roof of the dormitory full of cots, each cot surrounded by white mosquito netting attached to a hook on the ceiling above. The sister was carefully feeding a very young child she held in her arms. The child's small, almost limp body was clothed in a thin, white cotton T-shirt and light-brown corduroy pants that hung loosely, exposing emaciated ankles and feet and the stark, swollen belly symptomatic of starvation. The child's glazed eyes bulged. His shaved head was covered with nickel-size sores, a clear gluelike liquid oozing slightly from each wound, and a shimmering black halo of flies dancing and darting to strike at these wounds and the fluid they offered up. For now, the loving sister worked against poverty, disease, and eventual death, gently cradling and rocking the boy, and holding a small plastic syringe of water over the child's slack, open mouth. Drop by drop, as if in slow motion, she placed water in the child's mouth.

For the four US boys and me, the moment put us in touch with the harshest realities and challenges of the world that we were poised to enter, me as an educator, and them as young adults. Their response was illuminating, though not surprising. Confronted with a sight that would prompt many of us to turn away or give up, these boys were inspired to engage. Where we might expect them to recoil, they leaned in. Their first thoughts were about helping the sister give water to this boy; about doing more to help other orphans like this on that day and after; about coming back to Kigali and staying longer the next time to help more children like this young boy. This was a tipping point for those boys and for me. Until then, we had worked so hard. We had been exhausted at the end of each day. We had hoped that what we were able to do at Home of Hope in some way helped the orphans—young and old alike—and the sisters.

The boys' reactions of compassion, kindness, and engagement were not at all surprising in the face of one of the most disturbing realities the world has to offer. In nearly three decades of teaching foreign languages and preventive diplomacy skills to hundreds of students in middle and upper school classrooms worldwide, I have seen it time and again. Young peoples' desire to engage in the real world and to make a positive difference is inherent. By nature, children want to grow up to feel competent and connected, and to make some sort of an impact on the world around them. They have a phenomenal capacity to think critically, learn, care, imagine and innovate, take intellectual risks (often physical ones, too), and act on their intentions in ways that we in the adult world rarely acknowledge—or rarely do ourselves. Like my students who traveled to Rwanda and took part in our service-learning work there, most young people express their humanity naturally when invited to do so, especially if they have been raised in an environment where it is recognized and valued, encouraged from an early age, as, say, reading, writing, and sports skills are in most children's lives. The same natural curiosity, compassion, optimism, and energy that they bring to the world expand naturally across continents and cultures, if students are given a chance to go there.

By the time that Winston, Marcus, Burch, and Jake prepared to leave Rwanda three days after seeing that dear, sweet boy in the arms of the sister, they had already started thinking about returning to Rwanda the following summer, and how to recruit more of their US peers. Long after the trip ended, the four boys demonstrated to me that each, in his own way, had experienced a spiritual transformation. Each boy continued to keep in touch with the Rwandan students and families who had hosted them, through e-mail, phone, instant messaging, and Skype. The following fall, one of two twin brothers from a Kigali family that hosted us arrived in the United States to attend college in Newport, Rhode Island. On separate occasions, his US "brother" and I went to visit him, and when the new arrival came to Boston, this student from Rwanda came to visit our school, to expand his US circle of friends. The two students have not only kept in touch with each other, but deepened their friendship and continued their family-like conversations with growing interest and maturity. Both have maintained a sense of connection to the Kigali and the Boston communities. I have no doubt that the Rwandan student attending college in the United States, his friend here, and the other boys who made that trail-blazing first trip to Rwanda that summer are among the slowly growing group of globally street-smart future leaders of this country and of Rwanda. Each of those four boys wrote about his life-changing experience in Rwanda in his college essay. And Burch is now majoring in international relations and Arabic in college. I also have no doubt that whatever paths Winston, Marcus, Burch, and Jake eventually pursue after graduating from college, their educations and their hands-on experiences in their formative years have prepared them to think and act as global citizens—focused, informed, concerned, and purposeful—and improved their global IQs, too.

Students Without Borders: Serving Locally and Internationally

Of course, all students may not be able to travel halfway around the world to undertake service learning in a place like Rwanda, and in truth, they do not need to. Although the experience of the students who have visited the Home of Hope orphanage with me throughout the years—I have been there six times—has undeniably changed their entire outlook on the world, there are an infinite number of service-learning opportunities closer to home. Some of these opportunities may exist nationally and have other advantages besides reduced cost and easier logistics. One is the ability for students to get a rare window into their own history. But important opportunities exist locally as well. Every single community has concerns about poverty, disease, mental illness, homelessness, crime and violence, poor-quality education, loneliness, and neglect. Many have programs that can channel the energy of volunteers who want to make a difference; we just have to seek out these programs and establish these partnerships. Local service-learning exercises are also easier models for elementary and middle school students, while still being a wonderful way to prepare them more effectively for service-learning experiences farther away as they enter the advanced grades.

Whether a service-learning trip is local, national, or international, what makes the experience an effective lesson in global citizenship and improved global IQ is not so much the distance from home but rather that the work takes students out of their comfort zones and into new environments, many of which offer fresh views of other languages and other cultures. All involve different age groups, studies, interests, and destinations, but all have one common denominator: an experience that challenges students to step beyond what they have studied and what they know and who they think they are, and to put that newly acquired knowledge to work in the service of others. Upon returning to their schools, they should also be allowed to reflect on their experiences and share what they've learned, exciting their peers and setting the stage more effectively for future adventures that they and others may be willing to have. We need to take our children outside the classroom, the living room, the family room or the game room more often, and into the real world where they can meet unfamiliar people, encounter unfamiliar circumstances, and experience the challenges of new adventures in a well-thought-out, mature, and compassionate way.

We may teach K–12 students the importance of giving back, but we do them a disservice if we confine the lesson to the classroom, to talks around the dinner table, or at Sunday School. Outside, there is the global classroom around every corner, and if we take students there many times during their middle and high school years, the real world becomes more than the world of standardized exam scores, what colleges and graduate schools they get into, or the jobs and paychecks they imagine as the rewards of adult life. Instead, it becomes a wider arena of empathy, not apathy; of compassion, not complacency; of engagement and social responsibility, not disengagement and social detriment.

The Bible tells us, "For of those to whom much is given, much is required." In the next chapter of this book, I will explore some of the practical principles for organizing the kinds of experiential education service-learning programs that will work in your communities. I close this chapter with the words of Martin Luther King Jr., who saw the relevance of community service to the education of our children as responsible global citizens. In his 1968 sermon "The Drum Major Instinct," King said:

> Everybody can be great, because anybody can serve. You don't have to have a college degree to serve. You don't have to make your subject and your verb agree to serve. You don't have to know about Plato and Aristotle to serve. You don't have to know Einstein's theory of relativity to serve. You don't have to know the second theory of thermodynamics in physics to serve. You only need a heart full of grace, a soul generated by love.

CHAPTER NINE

PEARS: Five Key Aspects of Service Learning

We all know that life-changing epiphanies can happen immediately anywhere and without the benefit of a lesson plan. But when we talk about ways to upgrade education in order to improve our students' global IQ, well-developed service learning is one of the most dramatic and doable improvements we can make. It doesn't take an act of Congress or a majority vote at a meeting of a town's or city's school board. All we need is heartfelt desire, an openness to expanding the way we teach, and some sensitive and well-thought-out preparation to provide rich, hands-on opportunities to our students—and our own children.

Many schools and teachers involve their students in community-service activities on a regular basis or at various times during the year. Some schools even require a certain number of hours of community service per student or as a graduation prerequisite. Teachers and administrators who have kept in touch with me over the years have described in depth their efforts to upgrade these community-service endeavors, to make them quality service-learning experiences by expanding or deepening certain aspects of the projects through greater interdisciplinary collaboration in their schools. For example, Donna David, director of the Selma trip discussed in chapter 8, solicited the help of a US history teacher at her school in order to put together a good predeparture historical lesson plan. Other teachers have asked the technology department for assistance, using multimedia tools or other strategies focused on enhancing multicultural and global content to connect with people around the country or overseas involved in similar service-learning exercises; for example, connecting with doctors at Boston-based Partners In Health who are working at the new PIH clinic in the northwestern corner of Rwanda. US teachers' success stories and my own experiences suggest that there are five key aspects of quality service-learning programs that define students' experiences and can be fine-tuned for even richer possibilities. The five components can be easily remembered by using the acronym PEARS: preparation, engagement, action, reflection, and synthesis.

Preparation: A Review of Expectations and Information

Pre–service-learning preparatory study, information gathering with students rather than giving them lectures, and orientation exercises all generate content and context for the student. This is how students become knowledgeable about the exercise, practiced in skills they'll need for the service-learning activities, and emotionally prepared for them too. With so many exciting sources of information available through the Internet, students tend to be eager about this advance work. If they are allowed to play an active role in researching information and presenting findings prior to the beginning of the activity, they become research assistants and leaders in their own ways, an important component of this preparatory or preservice team-building exercise. Traditional library sources of information (books, magazines, and other print and audiovisual materials) are now part of a much larger array of sources and services in schools, technology or media centers, and school technology and media specialists are often enthusiastic advisers for teachers and students alike on the most current and trustworthy information sources geared to different age groups.

At this research and development—or R&D—phase of a quality service-learning project, expectations are as important as information to be gathered. This is the time to discuss preconceived ideas students may have about the people with or for whom they will be working, the place they are about to visit, or the work they will do once they get there. For example, a high school student who had volunteered for cleanup duty in Louisiana after Hurricane Katrina hit the Gulf Coast in 2005 was dismayed upon arrival to discover his team had been assigned to help in a wealthy area of New Orleans that had been demolished by the storm. He felt "poor people"—poor in more ways than one—needed the help more. For hours, he and his classmates shoveled rubble to the roadside in two different gated communities in New Orleans for the garbage truck crews to haul it away. At one point, he picked up an initialed, sterling silver napkin ring and set it by the tree where cleanup crews placed salvaged personal items so former residents could find them when they visited. Just then, an elderly woman approached the crew to thank them for their help. She explained that her family home was among those that had been completely destroyed, along with everything in it. The boy, nodding in understanding, showed her the napkin ring. She began to cry. It was hers, a wedding gift nearly a half-century before. If she had been asked what single material thing she would have chosen to save, she told the group, it would have been the napkin ring, for the years of memories it held for her. Later, as the students worked, they talked about what single material thing they would save if they knew all else was to be lost. While the question of relative need was still present, in the end, the conversation gave way to a realization of how little material things really matter and how much family, friends, and love matter more than anything, no matter one's socioeconomic background. So although he felt it was unfair to help the people in a gated community get back on their feet after the devastating hurricane, this boy discovered that he was able to give back to others. He would help to plan the next service-learning trip like this to ensure that others needing help would be both the "haves" and the "have-nots."

Depending on their age and life experience, students often have preconceived ideas and misconceptions about groups of people designated as needy, poor, disabled, or different in some way, as well as about the rich and famous and the pompous and self-centered. Some prejudices are based on nothing but stereotypes; others are based on an experience that students may have generalized to be true. For affluent students, especially, their firsthand experience of privilege may be expressed as a sense of entitlement or condescending noblesse oblige that allows them to cast themselves as charitable benefactors. This point of view, perhaps heard around many a dining room table in the suburbs, in the ski lodge, or in the beach resort restaurant, that implies a kind of moral or intellectual superiority based simply on financial resources, is important to address, too. Children face the task of overcoming a history of "Uncle Sam and the upwardly mobile know best." This culturally blind benevolence, insensitive in its ignorance, has wasted billions of dollars in aid for ventures that have disregarded essential aspects of recipient communities, such as those hardest hit by Hurricane Katrina, and at times have only made conditions worse. But today's higher quality service-learning programs incorporate knowledge, understanding, respect, and appreciation of other cultures' strengths and dignity as key lessons, and their planners and executors realize that excellent preparation is a key component.

Other preconceptions of a simpler, more practical nature—imagining what the work will be like and what conditions the students will discover—can often be more educational and, at times, more amusing than concerning. When students include thoughts about these points in preservice journals or essays, it can be illuminating later to compare the actual experience with the notions they had earlier. For example, one boy, before leaving for Rwanda, wondered if he should bring his own favorite candy and granola bars, thinking that he would not have much food when he arrived. He was surprised to discover, after helping his host mother kill a chicken that they ate for dinner an hour later, that his preconceived notions were not true.

Finally, parents are often overlooked in the preparation of service-learning activities, but that shortchanges team efforts to create the strongest possible base of support for teaching global responsibility. Parents are usually eager or at least willing to be more involved in this exciting educational process, to hear from the service-learning experience planner and visiting speakers, or to contribute in ways that allow them to support service-learning work and their children's commitment. By inviting and promoting parent support of service-learning activities in the lower grades and implementing the simplest activities in the school or local community, we build the team base of interest and support for wide-ranging or more ambitious programs, including eventual international travel for older students. Think about inviting parents on these life-changing service-learning trips, as well. This parent-child connection—from trip preparation to working together on a common goal during the trip—can completely and positively change how parents and their children relate to one another. As mentor Roger Fisher always said to me, "This will be a win-win situation!"

Engagement: First Impressions, Lasting Lessons

Navy SEALS and US Army special forces officers put their recruits through grueling training exercises to bring them to the point of complete mental and physical exhaustion and vulnerability: the military's version of the ultimate teachable moment. In service-learning activities, that "Wow, do I get it now" moment of truth—laced with vulnerability and openness—arrives when students step into a new environment and come face-to-face with the people or problems that need their assistance. This moment of truth may arrive through a five-year-old girl crying nonstop at the sight of her reading mentor, who is a middle school student and who has just walked through the door of her classroom to begin a weekly extra help session. It may be at the first sight of a devastated New Orleans neighborhood from the window of the bus as out-of-town high school students arrive to assist in disaster cleanup in a community hit by Hurricane Katrina. Students have shared stories of "the moment it hit me" when they walked through the airport after an international flight, stepped out into the daylight of the city where they would be volunteering, and were slammed by a wall of heat, crowds, beggars, and unfamiliar language, as well as a potpourri of sights, sounds, and smells that shocked their senses to the core. Or they arrived with grim expectations that locals who would look down upon them as evil people from the West, only to be swept instead into the welcoming embraces of hosts whose simple warmth and vibrant conversation changed everything—hitting the student's mental reset button. This shock, awe, surprise, and personal transformation convey the amazing power of service learning, locally, nationally, or internationally, one student at a time.

Vulnerability—the moment when the veneer of preconceptions and walls of defense mechanisms crack and defenses are down—opens us to receive and to absorb new experiences and extraordinary new learning possibilities effectively. That's true for any of us, but especially so for young people. Students—if taught to be open, honest, smart, fair, direct, and transparent—as I have found for almost thirty years, open their souls, often in ways that surprise the adults with them. I can remember moments when I was caught off-guard by some snag in a travel plan or an unplanned circumstance. While I put my mind to fixing what I perceived as a problem, my students had already accepted the problem, moved through it, and advanced on to creative ways of biding the time, not stressing about the situation. On one trip to Rwanda, I found out that some of my students and I had a nine-hour layover in Addis Ababa (Ethiopia) International Airport before our connecting flight departed for Kigali, Rwanda. Sensing my evident dismay, one of the boys, my amazing nephew, said to me, "Carl, you have your OMG! [Oh my God!] face on. How about putting on your NBD! [No big deal!] face? We'll camp out over there on the floor of the terminal and play a poker tournament. Okay, boss?" He and the other students' intuitive response—and this can take place in a matter of seconds—was to *deal with it*, bond as a team, help each other out, and pitch in to help others who were stressed out . . . like *me*! Whether it is a situational surprise such as a long flight layover, a dramatic moment of culture shock when first entering the Home of Hope orphanage in Kigali, or a simple chance encounter—stepping off the bus at a house in Alabama and seeing the amount of work to be done, for instance—students come through this "reset" experience quickly and effectively, with a boost in team-play mentality, self-confidence and a sprinkle of humility. Their momentary experiences of openness and vulnerability have the unconscious effect of making them more empathetic to others' vulnerability as well. They have come to that edge of the cliff themselves, they are able to quickly react in a positive way, and they are able to relate to it in their own way, however unconsciously, when they meet vulnerability in others face-to-face.

Action: Discovering the Power to Make a Difference

If the initial encounter confronts students with the question, "Who do I need to be in order to be effective in this moment?" then the core service-learning activity is where they find their answer. The action in question may reflect the teachers' and organizers' understanding of the mission and the task at hand, but it is the students' individual responses and actions that keep the action fresh, original, and permanently imprinted in their porous minds. And every student's success—the mass of experiences, ideas, insights, and imagination that emerges from the hands-on work—contributes to the overall experience of the group as well.

If you could capture the moment of personal transformation in slow motion or time-lapse photography, this is how it would look: the initial preparation, the often shallow level of confidence, the butterflies in the stomach, the white-water rafting flow of adrenaline, the rapid heartbeat, then the shock of the "new," followed by the overwhelming sense of powerlessness and confusion about how to deal with it. The immediate, catalyzing cry for help from outside their shocked interior, then the insistent call to action, and, to their own surprise, their instinctive, positive response and their ability to "feel the fear, and do it anyway," succeeding in the end. And, as I have witnessed countless times before, all this may happen in a matter of seconds. This is conflict analysis, management and prevention practice on the most intimate scale: How do you deal with a situation that throws you for an unbelievably intense loop? What action do you take to respond quickly and effectively when what is being demanded of you is more than you feel able to do? How do you shift gears inside your soul in order to go from feeling stuck, shackled, behind bars, to moving forward and, in doing so, discovering your power to help others?

The content of every moment—the action, thought, and feeling we see as an experience that imprints itself on our brains, in what is known as direct learning—is shaped by many factors on the ground, in the planning, in the student's expectations and experience, and in the execution of the experience. But whether the activity is on your own campus, at a local soup kitchen nearby, a veterans' hospital a day's ride away, a devastated area of the United States, or an orphanage halfway around the world, every student eventually finds the answer; every student "gets it" about helping others and helping themselves and about the relationship between these two. In this intense activity, there is no "I am doing this to get into college" and there is no way to fail. Interestingly, those whom I have found to engage more easily and quickly are often students who have younger siblings at home (or siblings with disabilities) or those who have had to learn how to manage conflict successfully as part of family life, living through, for example, a divorce or the death of a parent. Regardless of family size or situation, however, students who have learned conflict analysis, management, and prevention skills, and how to apply these skills to everyday life find they can draw on that knowledge to become what we might call "humble cultural chameleons," able to blend in, engage, adapt, and thrive assisting others in diverse settings, which often conflict with their own—socially, economically, and politically.

Reflection: Home Again, the Same but Different

Reflection is one way we process experience, giving it meaning, context, and coherence. In reflection, the seemingly small events of the day can take on greater meaning, and we can begin to break the big events into manageable pieces, seizing them like a Venus flytrap, and digesting them over time. That's the incredible essence of learning. This is especially important in improving the global intelligence quotient of children, too. In the global arena, the impact of our choices and actions on youth isn't always instantly apparent; in fact, it rarely is. But our ability to pause and reflect on uncomfortable or confusing situations gives us a chance to practice thinking before acting and leads to making smarter decisions, including how to teach our students and our children. A woman named Ellen, a kindergarten teacher for thirty-five years, once told me that she attempted to counter the fast-paced, overpackaged, media-driven lives of her young students by "teaching them to ponder." She included periods for reflection in the children's school day and found it made for more thoughtful, interesting class discussions and, for some, had a helpful calming effect. As I sat in the middle of several of these circle discussions, I asked the children to ponder, "If you knew that people were homeless and not eating, and they lived near your school, what would you do?" Their responses still bring tears to my eyes: "I would bring food that my mom made to them in the shelter." "I would ask my father to buy a bag of groceries for them the next time we go to the supermarket. Then I'll deliver it." Students of all ages come to the exercise of reflection with different ways of processing information and emotions, and different ways of expressing themselves. But what's important is that we create the opportunity for and offer guidance in the quiet art of reflection. Their ideas can be true jewels.

The results can be gratifying, too. Students sometimes surprise themselves with their own insights, and the opportunity to share their reflections deepens their learning experience. Donna David, whom we met in the previous chapter, points to the immediate effect her students describe after working in Alabama, as well as with special needs children and adults in their own community. After even one such experience in which her students played field games with severely physically disabled children, she recalls, "One of my students told me, 'Before we went, when I'd pass a kid like that on the sidewalk, I just walked past. Now I say, 'Hi, how are you?''" This same student was one of the first to step forward for the service-learning trip to Selma.

Often, when the service-learning experience is deeply affecting, the reflections offer a way to capture the raw sensory experience, the mélange of action, thought, and feeling to which they can return and reflect anew to find new meaning in past experiences. One of my "gang of four" students from the Rwanda trip, Marcus, now at Trinity College in Connecticut, kept a journal during his trip. Some excerpts on his experience at the Home of Hope orphanage describe his experience while there, in this case, learning about the Rwandan genocide:

KIGALI, RWANDA, JUNE 2007

Day One:

Left house at 7 a.m. to go to the Home of Hope Orphanage. . . . Didn't know what to expect. . . . Took a taxi to the church. . . . Realized that I was standing where innocent people's blood had been spilt, and where some of the genocide had occurred 13 years prior. . . .

We walked down the hill to the orphanage. . . . The walls around are topped with shards of broken glass in cement acting like barbed wire. . . . When we arrived and entered the front door, a sister came out to greet us. She was dressed like Mother Teresa. . . . We gave her our gifts from the US—children's clothing and diapers—and then were given a tour of the orphanage.

The living conditions for these children were horrible. . . . The door opened and there was a terrible stench of feces and urine. . . . Walking down the hall one and two year olds sitting in the hallway . . . smiling and talking and yelling to us. . . . Their faces light up with happiness.

Continued down the hallway to the nursery . . . filled with cribs with metal bars and such. . . . About 50 cribs stuffed into this small room each full of small babies smiling up at me. . . . I dangled my camera strap for one of the little ones and he loved it and giggled and just lied on his back smiling up at me and just observing what I was doing. . . . I usually have a talent for making babies smile, but one little boy gave me a run for my money. . . . But after a few strategically placed tickles and a funny face, I had him smiling and laughing.

Moved on outside to the toddlers in the play ground area. . . . Gates opened and the kids came running out in a stampede. . . . It then struck me: These kids have absolutely NOTHING, no parents, no real home, yet they are happy. Happier than most people I see back in the states. These children know no different. The poverty-laced orphanage they live in is their world, and they know nothing better. They take nothing for granted because most of the time they do not have anything to take for granted. Their happiness is in the purest, simplest form, and that is in love and affection. That is all that these children want. Love and affection. Sure: food, diapers, and toys can make these children happy, but deep down all they need is love.

It's truthfully the little things that make these children happy. . . . I lent this little girl my sunglasses, and she put them on and ran about showing all the other little ones. . . .

We walked further down to where the adults were . . . all direct victims of the genocide. . . . One woman was so traumatized/beaten/raped that she can barely hear and cannot see you. . . . She touches your hand and smells you to recognize your presence. . . .

I find it terrifying what people will do to each other. . . . The fact that someone can bring himself to rape and beat someone till near death when they have done nothing wrong and are just an innocent woman, man or child.

Day Two:

Winston and I took the toddlers and played with them and fed them. . . . They all wanted to be picked up and played with, which caused problems. . . . One girl fell asleep on my shoulder, and would not allow me to put her down. . . . All she would do was cry if I tried to put her down. . . . Again, it struck me that all these kids are happy. . . . It truly made me realize how lucky I am to even have a family, a wonderful, kind and caring family. . . . We went down to the lower levels of the orphanage. . . . Came across a sister holding a little five year old child . . . HIV+ . . . 5 months to live maybe . . .

Here we are, fussing about the little things such as if our car does not start or if we do not get our food on time in a restaurant, while there is a 5-year-old child whose life is hanging on a thread, and sadly a thread that will most likely break very soon. . . .

Possibly the saddest thing I have ever seen. . . .

Another day of the trip we went to a church that was halfway between Kigali and Burundi [a neighboring country, to the south of Rwanda]. . . . Genocide killings took place inside the church, and it is left as it was in 1994. . . . There is a heart made out of bricks in the front garden of the church. . . . Bullet holes appear in the door because it was shot open. . . . Stepped inside . . . there are bones lying about as a reminder of how horrible it was. . . . Bullet holes in the ceiling. . . . Skulls of children and women who were raped and beaten to death. . . . People came to the church because they thought it was a place of refuge. . . . They were butchered inside this House of God. . . .

Again I still wonder what has the world come to. . . . What can draw someone to brutally rape and beat an innocent man, woman or child. . . . I just don't understand how one can force oneself to do such a thing.

Another day, we went to the Genocide Museum, which was back in Kigali. . . . The museum told stories of people, about how they lost their families and also told survivor stories. . . . Some of them are so graphic and so vile that I feel awkward sometimes telling people about them, but I feel it is necessary to tell the world, to show the world what destruction is going on, and how we are often doing nothing about it.

For instance . . . a woman was telling her story about how men came to their house, and took her father outside, and cut off his head and gutted him right in front of her, her mother and her brothers and sisters. . . . Her mother was then raped and beaten to death and her little brother and sister [only about 2 or 3 years old] were thrown into a septic tank and drowned. . . . The girl was then raped and beaten into a state that was almost irrecoverable. . . . This is just a taste of how violent and horrible the genocide in Rwanda was. . . .

The next day, went back to HOH [Home of Hope] and worked with the little ones again. . . . Had a little boy who would not stop crying and would not allow me to put him down. . . . Got him to fall asleep on my shoulder. . . . Was allowed to take a picture of him [usually, no photos are allowed]. . . . Put him down in his bed and covered him with a blanket. . . . A sister told me how he came to them. . . . He was found in the toilet bowl of a broken toilet that had been thrown in a ditch. . . . Most of the children in the orphanage are just left outside the gate of the orphanage, in the middle of the night.

Trip Overview

I haven't had a legitimate shower in 9 days. . . . People in the USA/ Rest of the World do not understand how lucky they are to take 1, 2 or 3 showers or more each day. . . . This truly has been a life changing experience. . . . I will never be the same.

So long as you have somebody to love, and somebody to love you, you are beyond lucky. . . . Truly, just spending a few hours every day at the orphanage made a world of difference to these kids. . . . Just a smile made a difference to them. . . . I may not have a clue how to say anything in Kinyarwanda, but every little child in the orphanage, every adult, every man woman and child in Rwanda, everyone in the entire WORLD, understands the meaning of a smile. Why don't we smile more often?

We know as teachers that the K–12 years can be tricky. Students often feel they have little opportunity to articulate or share their deepest emotions with their families, their peers, or even themselves. Most of their educators, peers, and people in their lives in general discourage them from such disclosure, from such vulnerability. The exercise of personal and private reflection creates a psychologically safe place for students to open up, show their emotions, and acknowledge what they've been through. Debriefing with themselves and others gives a student a chance to compare notes and memories while they're still fresh. It's important to get those words down, whether in a journal, an essay, a poem, a song, e-mails, a Facebook page, or a blog. This makes the experience come alive to them while still fresh, so that they may reexperience it from a new perspective and in reflection later when they learn from the experience again.

Synthesis: Transforming Experience into New Possibilities

Wherever a service-learning activity has taken students and whatever the focus of their work, I find that they return with a kind of missionary zeal for telling others about it. It makes no sense to end a transformative experience and, in effect, say, "Yes, I'm back now. This is school. I'll forget all that and turn to page 63 for tomorrow's assignment." Sharing the experience with a wide audience, and not returning completely to the gerbil wheel of memorization and regurgitation of information, is a mechanism for continuing to serve and learn. Hence, we must provide opportunities for students to debrief, reflect, and to put their experiences into words and remember and learn from them. If we want children's education to transition from knowledge to insight and then to responsible and thoughtful action, we need to give them opportunities to learn how to practice those skills.

One teacher, who is also the community-service coordinator for her school, describes the challenge:

> Because of the ever-present issue of time constraints in schools, we often do not have a good forum in which to share the adventures of our trips with the community as a whole. We do have group dinners following our trips, at which time all of the families are present, and that is always a lot of fun and very informative for everyone. I believe that the stories the students have to tell, along with the photos of the trip, would go a long way to inspiring others in the community to want to do the same. . . . I do think and know that the school is "proud" of the fact that we do this kind of thing [the trips], but I wish there were a better way to debrief when we return—a better way to share these experiences with others in the community.

Many teachers have their students prepare written reports on their service-learning experiences; some have students present the reports to different classes. Sometimes a student will write a feature article for the school newspaper or other publication that reaches the school community. Other times, students step into the teacher role in the classroom to give a short speech or lecture on the core ideas of the service-learning program. When returnees take to the podium to show a video of the trip or to give a talk, naturally their classmates are rapt.

When Donna David's students returned from the Selma experience, for example, they were impassioned about bringing a greater awareness of the trip and of diversity issues to their own school. Several of the participants approached members of the administration about not only speaking to the school community about the trip but also doing something related to the trip that went beyond this all-school presentation. They hoped to declare a full school day devoted to diversity studies, including student- and faculty-directed workshops and lectures by guest speakers. They were told that if they could build a good program, it would be done—and that's exactly what they did. The students organized the school's first Diversity Day, timed around Black History Month, and it is now an annual event. Their inaugural speaker: none other than the Reverend Dr. Frederick D. Reese from Selma, Alabama.

The Impact of Service Learning on Global IQ

Donna David feels that the work ethic and dedication engendered by a service-learning experience can extend into the college and post-college years, as well. "Service-learning trips educate the students to become better, more compassionate human beings," David says. "Endeavors like this impact the kind of person you are, the kind of father or mother you're going to be, the kind of partner you're going to be, the kind of worker you may be in whatever workforce you go into, bringing integrity and respect and care to other people around you."

If we want our children to think with a service-learning mind-set and to connect it to thinking globally, we need to model that kind of thinking ourselves. If we want them to move easily into opportunities for global interaction, service learning rather than tourist travel, and quality study abroad, we need to provide ways for students to practice skills to engage comfortably with new people, places, and ideas. It isn't that hard. You don't have to fly across oceans to experience being a stranger in a strange land. In the United States today, children live vastly different lives sometimes within blocks of each other. Even within the same school, students from different family backgrounds or socioeconomic circumstances can be involved in activities that help them learn more deeply about the diversity in their midst.

Look for parallels between those local issues and those occurring in a larger or perhaps more severe way in other places: invite a local rabbi, minister, priest, and imam to take part in a panel discussion, during which they discuss the rising tensions between Israel and Iran, the elections in Egypt, or the revolution taking place in Syria. Invite graduates of your school who have gone on to pursue global careers to reflect on why they did so and how they got to where they are now. Invite an area professor to come to campus or to speak via Skype about environmental degradation, and the pluses and minuses of proposed wind turbine farms. Use these unique, creative teaching moments as a way for students and educational communities to study and learn about sources of conflict and conflict management and prevention. Issues of religious conflict, poverty, bigotry, poor nutrition and health care, violence, and the exploitation of individuals in the workplace or domestic settings are painfully present across the United States. The more opportunities students have to study, work, eat, play, live, breathe, and communicate about these and other hot-button issues, the more profoundly educated and culturally literate they become. Whatever their socioeconomic circumstances—privileged or disadvantaged alike—these educational experiences allow them to transcend limiting assumptions and develop the critical thinking and personal interaction skills vital to success in local, regional, national, and global communication, collaboration, compassion—and more peaceful coexistence.

As Edward Everett Hale wrote in his poem "Lend a Hand," "I am only one; but still I am one. I cannot do everything; but still I can do something; and because I cannot do everything, I will not refuse to do the something that I can do." Ultimately, this is the simple and profound lesson of service learning: students, led by their teachers, advisers, mentors, and parents discovering their own power to make a difference, to do something, anything to make a small, positive change in this rapidly shrinking world. Local and regional field trips, service-learning trips, and cross-cultural exchanges with diverse segments of the community are all accessible in every community. Interest in service learning among all age groups, including middle school, high school, and college students, young professionals, parents (sometimes with their own children), and active retirees, has led to a proliferation of programs and sponsoring organizations. I've listed some that might interest you in the resources section at the end of this book. It's important to note, however, that some of the best resources and partners can be found through other educators, parents, businesspeople, and other leaders in local communities whose passion for service learning and creativity will lead to rich possibilities and extraordinary results. When you ponder these resource ideas, take the time to talk with people outside your inner circle of friends and colleagues. Students, too, often have the best ideas. Your expression of respect for others—like your students—and your enthusiasm for expansive networking and collaborative partnering make an excellent model of global responsibility for young people. Carpe diem.

PART THREE

BUILDING THE GLOBAL IQ INFRASTRUCTURE AT YOUR SCHOOL

CHAPTER TEN

Global IQ and the Architecture of Educational Transformation

Dramatic change in US K–12 education to improve the global IQ of K–12 students is possible when we all know enough and care enough to make it a top priority, from the halls of the US Department of Education in Washington, DC, to classrooms, dining room tables, and family rooms. When we realized the importance of technology, we began integrating it across academic disciplines to enhance what and how we taught our youth. We also experienced a period of education renaissance with the arrival of that complex, multifaceted word *diversity*. With the advent of the diversity discussion, we began to rethink how we would teach our students about African American, Native American, Chinese American, or Arab American history and peoples and so much more. We began to teach younger and younger students about people with sexual differences and people of myriad socioeconomic classes, so that educating about diversity became a new and important goal of US K–12 educators. Once we knew about and cared enough about major issues like technology, diversity, or even the newer concept of environmental sustainability, change became the order of the day. The question wasn't "whether" but "how?" and "how fast?"

While I have spent the better part of this book (and my personal life) asserting that we can and must do a better job boosting our students' global IQ, I know at the same time that we will do so successfully only if we begin to work on it *now* as a team of teachers, administrators, parents, and students, not in our own separate educational fiefdoms. Many schools have embarked on the path of global education: teaching global literacy and global citizenship skills through increased foreign language course offerings, overseas travel, guest speakers, and more. But many of these schools have not shared their findings with other schools or collaborated with them. If we want more schools—and more students—to be able to navigate this new educational frontier, we must work together, creating as a team of educators and parents more advanced training and tools so that the broad curricular expanse of education, and improving the concept of global IQ, becomes a beacon of hope for our students and our children, now and for decades to come.

Of course, the actual architecture of such educational transformation varies widely among US public, private, and parochial schools, and even among different schools within those groups, from elementary to middle and high schools. Conditions in American international schools abroad are quite diverse also, and no single blueprint will work for all. There is the incredible, rapidly growing International Baccalaureate program too. With host schools across the United States and abroad, IB includes three separate programs, for students ages three to nineteen, to help prepare them to live, learn, and work effectively in a rapidly shrinking world. Founded in 1968, IB offers challenging programs to over a million students, helping them to develop intercultural understanding and respect. According to its mission statement, the International Baccalaureate aims "to develop inquiring, knowledgeable and caring young people . . . who understand that other people, with their differences, can also be right."

Beyond IB schools, and whether in Boston, San Francisco, or Kigali, every school or school district has factors—demographics, budgets, community resources, challenges from a variety of interest groups—that will influence and shape the way they move forward to improve their school's global IQ. In my work with a diverse array of schools and communities and age groups, I have found that the measures offered in this book form a core curriculum of what can be done to initiate a program meant to improve global IQ. My goal has been to provide a road map for teachers and administrators, parents, and students, as they look for ways to boost global IQ in classrooms, schools, districts, homes, neighborhoods, and communities.

However, one crucial common denominator I have found is the necessity of at least one passionate proselytizer of a school's or district's efforts to "go global." Schools and entire districts have directors of technology and directors of diversity; now, they need a new kind of talented team captain to the educational team: a director of global programs.

Director of Global Programs

Each successive wave in education benefited from having a talented point person, either someone overseeing several schools from a district position or a person who had this role, as a faculty member within an individual school. There to guide us through the explosive possibilities of the new media and electronic toolkit was the director of technology. We turned to the director of diversity to help us embrace and blend effectively the richness of our distinctive heritages. In the case of the oncoming (or already present) wave of globalization, we need to be able to turn to an individual who will help inspire, organize, and mobilize our efforts in globalizing across the curriculum, in many academic departments and extracurricular activities.

In this book, I call such a person the director of global programs, although you may also see such titles as director of global education or international studies. Regardless of the exact title, the role remains constant—to be the point guard of the school's or community's globalization efforts, to get the word out to an entire school or local community along each educational spoke I have been discussing (foreign languages, technology, etc.) about the importance of globalization. The director—for example, a well-traveled, multilingual modern language teacher, an English teacher who spent time in the Peace Corps, a history teacher who offers an excellent and popular global issues course—should engage colleagues in every discipline: the foreign language educators; the history teachers who teach Middle East, African, or world history courses; the arts instructors who take their students to museums; the sports coaches; those who can coordinate community service and experiential learning on a local, national, or international level; and so many more members of the school community. In addition, the director of global programs can and must reach beyond the academic community to canvass with other members of the school's or district's community: administrators, parents, alumni, board members, and community leaders such as business owners, philanthropists, and politicians. At the same time, the director must galvanize the single most important resource for globalizing a school—the students themselves. It is not an easy job. But with some foresight (and this book aims to contribute to this), the director of global programs can help a school improve its global IQ and prevent it from failing in its attempt to do so.

There are currently many different routes to take in becoming a director of global programs. One director I know is also the chair of the history department at his school; he is not fluent in another language but he combines his law degree and excellent US history curriculum with a passion for his students' progress in grasping threatening geopolitical realities. Another director is a former English teacher who did not start out with much international experience, but embraced the foreign travel component of her job with gusto and is now an expert on orchestrating "transformative service-learning trips of a lifetime" at very low cost. A third director is an excellent foreign language teacher; having already developed her global street smarts and her empathy from being a transplant to this country herself, she is now enjoying professional growth as an administrator, coordinating a variety of globalization efforts in the United States and abroad while based at her Texas school.

My point is that how one learns to take on the role of director of global programs can be quite individual: someone may have Peace Corps training or a background in the US military, based overseas, another may simply be an excellent, seasoned, veteran teacher looking for a new challenge that comes from his or her perception of the necessity of globalization. Yet another may be a veteran modern language teacher who has taught French, Spanish, or Mandarin Chinese for years, and has taken countless student groups abroad; for her or him, this is a logical next step in a fascinating career as an educator. Learning to play the role of director of global programs *well* is another matter. As I have seen in successful models, it is always achieved by jumping in with both feet and embracing the opportunity with maximum integrity and minimal fear, and with a carefully researched and written plan. At this stage of the relatively young global IQ game, that may be all we have.

One concrete personality characteristic of a good director of global programs is the ability to think quickly on his or her feet, and to build consensus for new and different program ideas, especially with colleagues who may be unable to make what Chip and Dan Heath call for in their book *Switch: How to Change Things When Change Is Hard*. As I have found for nearly thirty years, educators frequently ask: "How are we going to be able to find the time to globalize our curricula?" "Our academic clock is not broken! Why should we fix it?" But in order to embrace this challenge of globalization head on, it is first necessary to determine which parts of a school or which members of its community are willing to allow their members to develop a more global perspective and are themselves already educating for a global community. Those aspects, whether individuals or departments, must be brought together to create a critical mass, however small, to truly allow the globalization of the curriculum to begin to grow. While encouraging these areas or methods for increasing global literacy through academic classes and extracurricular activities, the director must also learn to include some of the recalcitrant corners of her or his academic world. Just as there were educators who were resistant to technology and then to the complex, often difficult-to-define and fraught idea of diversity, some members of a school community will see globalization as just another fad. But I believe that slowly and subtly, even these folks' minds can be changed, one teacher at a time, just as technology arrived and succeeded in changing teachers' minds years ago. Why not take a skeptical teacher, coach, or administrator with you on your next service-learning trip, working with disadvantaged children across town at a shelter for homeless children or halfway across the world in a foreign country? Why not invite a geography teacher to bring her or his classes to a guest speaker's lecture on Peru's Machu Picchu? These consensus-building ideas are endless. The director should also be included in monthly meetings of the Committee on Academic Policy (CAP) or Academic Policy Committee (APC) with administrators and department chairpersons, as well as in weekly meetings of the team of top administrators.

Another way for the director to build consensus is to put together his or her own globalization steering committee, and to make the goals and procedures open, transparent, and accessible. Such a steering committee might include other teachers, administrators, members of the school board and/or the board of trustees, parents, students, alumni, and other community members. In this way, members of the entire school community can become involved in the brainstorming exercise, decision-making process, and eventual oversight and promotion of both established and possible globalization efforts, and they can become liaisons to other interest groups in the process, as well.

Points of Inquiry for a Director of Global Programs

That I believe deeply in the philosophy of global intelligence should come as no surprise. I'm fervent about it and come to this subject as a teacher myself. Through my nonprofit organization, Axis of Hope, and my individual consulting, I travel extensively promoting the idea of boosting a school's global IQ and working with directors of global programs worldwide. I have also compiled some common questions I ask directors, so that they may then assess their school's position on the global IQ spectrum and move forward. The answers are sometimes simple and sometimes complex—and how the answers or recommendations are used may depend on funding, department or school goals, mission statements of the school, and so on. But throughout, we must always remember two things: (1) we must ask these questions of the entire community; and (2) we must be interested in doing something today, rather than waiting until a certain piece is in place or a perfect plan is authorized to start globalization efforts.

Questions about Foreign Languages

- Does your school hire a combination of US-born foreign language instructors who have learned the language(s) that they teach as a foreign tongue and native speakers who have learned English as a foreign language in order to teach foreign language courses more effectively as teams? If possible, a school should provide both. In this way, students can learn from both native and US-born fluent speakers offering language courses. As I mentioned earlier, both types of teachers have fluency in the target language. They also have an understanding of and empathy for those learning a second language.

- What types of foreign language classes are offered—and at what ages do students begin these? It is important to evaluate currently existing foreign language programs and to decide if others, such as Arabic, should be offered and, if so, if one or more currently offered language programs, such as French, German, Russian, or Japanese, for example, should be closed.

- How are those people who offer the language courses—both native speakers and those who have learned the language(s) well as a second language—evaluated? Do they pursue professional growth and development opportunities regularly to keep up to date with the latest language pedagogy (such as regional and national conferences, including the American Council on the Teaching of Foreign Languages [ACTFL])?

- What summer school opportunities exist for foreign language teachers and for middle and upper school students, especially, to continue their study of foreign languages? (Two excellent language programs are listed in the resources section in the back of this book. There are more.) Have interested students and parents join you in researching all the incredible summer language possibilities.

Questions about Technology

- Are technology and media literacy used to enhance not only foreign language study but all classes, connecting students to people and ideas from other parts of the world at the touch of a keyboard? In other words, is technology being used to enhance and globalize all courses, bringing the world into the classroom in some kind of creative way, every day?
- Is Skype or advanced videoconferencing used regularly to bring experts (virtually) or students' peers from other parts of the world into the classroom?

Questions about Extracurricular Activities, Service Learning, and Foreign Travel

- Are class groups, sports teams, bands, choirs, acting groups, school newspaper groups, and so on participating in service-learning programs in the United States and possibly abroad to form another kind of team, working together toward a common goal of helping others?
- Does your school plan service-learning trips that reflect the increasingly globalized education offered at your school? And are these trips reasonably priced, or does your school offer financial aid to ensure access to students of all socioeconomic backgrounds who wish to participate?
- Are these trips truly service-learning-based—or do they provide only short, quick-fix, drive-by service-learning opportunities and are actually more tourist-oriented trips?
- Do hands-on, educationally enriching, service-learning opportunities for students already exist, not just possibilities in a folder on a desk somewhere?
- Do these possibilities exist locally, regionally, nationally—and globally? How many students and teachers are actually participating in these valuable service-learning-based programs each year?

- Has there been discussion about how faculty members—who may be exhausted and need downtime during their school vacations—can go on trips in a way that will delight and not exhaust them even more? And if this is possible, how can they be compensated?
- Does your school have a mechanism by which it can admit foreign students to enrich the school culture for a full academic year; a semester, trimester, or quarter; or even a short portion of the year in, for example, a carefully planned student exchange program? Such programs provide both students and the community at large an opportunity to befriend students and teachers from other cultures in their own schools, thereby encouraging an awareness of the need for greater tolerance and understanding of others—and creating an increased desire to explore beyond the confines of the school walls.
- Are there off-campus service-learning possibilities that reflect the increasingly globalized education offered at your school?

Questions about the Case-Study Curriculum

- In any of your school's classes, is "preventive diplomacy," as described earlier in the book, being taught?
- Is a Global Issues course being taught in your school?
- Is the increasingly important—and accepted—intellectual Outward Bound, case-study approach to education used, and in how many disciplines? Example: a case study focusing on the increasingly hot debate over wind turbines off Cape Cod in Massachusetts.
- Has your school been able to create programs with other students for students to engage in preventive diplomacy or similar case-study-based role-play exercises?
- Has your school created programs, seminars, or opportunities for faculty and/or students from your and other schools to

learn more about the preventive diplomacy model by participating in these exercises?

- Would you like to become a member of an international Axis of Hope global IQ online support group, so that new ideas might be exchanged, both now and for years to come? In this way, we'll be able to keep this process of improving global IQ moving forward together. Teachers, administrators, parents, and students: share the positive changes that have been made and the improvement in global IQ in our communities. The address: info@axisofhope.org.

Once we recognize the importance of improving global IQ in our schools, we must then motivate school communities to blaze a trail and rethink and refine this trail regularly. Rather than being bogged down by what I call "analysis paralysis," always looking for inevitable bumps in the road, we must continue to search for and advertise the bright spots along the way—the success stories of individual teachers, administrators, parents, and students inspired to take action. Together we can assess what has worked and how to copy it, and what has not worked and how to alter it, as we spread these valuable lessons effectively over time through this new support group.

We, as teachers and parents, have our students and our children to work with and to love, in their formative years. We must remember their power: they can develop native fluency in foreign languages much more effectively than we can. We turn to them when we have problems with our iPhones or MacBook Pros or cable television remote control devices. When, as in these simple examples, we show that we trust our youth and give them the opportunity to step outside the box of standard educational boundaries in order to cultivate their own new, creative thoughts, improved self-confidence soars along with improved global IQ. When we give them new educational opportunities, they are eager to take the reins and proceed. When we allow them to live and breathe other languages and cultures, and to study profoundly the successes and failures of other peoples, today and in history, they learn to become humble chameleons who can astutely and positively react to problems in their own lives and in the lives of those across town or around the world.

As we teach youth critical thinking, problem solving, creativity, collaboration, agility, and adaptation, we show them empathy and compassion, and they learn to bring these important characteristics more effectively to others, too. They feel compassion for the seven-year-old girl in their town who has been taken away from her parents by the Department of Social Services because she was being abused, and they donate their time tutoring her after school. They learn the importance of a high school senior spring vacation trip to rebuild Habitat for Humanity homes in New Orleans, rather than to join college-bound friends on a booze cruise in Mexico. They become magnets to little three and four year olds in the Home of Hope orphanage in Rwanda, as they pull a long wooden bench up to the crib to feed the children porridge, rather than spending the entire summer on a Cape Cod beach.

Youth can be so compassionate, so caring. And they can process so quickly how to show these traits, when we give them the reins and stand aside as their inspirational teachers and coaches and wise mentors. As more of us give these reins to more wonderful youth, I find hope for improved global IQ in US K–12 students, and a better future in our rapidly shrinking world. We and our youth together form the world's Axis of Hope. And spinning around this Axis of Hope is a world that can, living by a universal code of compassion, be more empathetic and more caring. As we encourage US schools and communities to pursue improved global IQ, we define a new horizon in US education as well: to bring the world to the class, and the class to the world. The decision is ours. Do we bring needed, more globally focused change to US education slowly, like the drip of water from an eye dropper? Or do we instead, as a team of parents, teachers, school administrators, and students, embrace the idea of educational transformation leading to improved global IQ and run with it? I believe we must do the latter, creating in the end a more supportive, interconnected community of care in our homes, our schools, and our country. After all, it is all about the kids, remember?

Acknowledgments

The successful completion of this book took almost thirty years of research, teaching, coaching, advising, and parenting. And it took over six years to complete—yes, six years after I signed the contract with Beacon Press! During this time, I have been very fortunate to work with truly amazing people who have helped me throughout to complete this written work. To them and to many more whom I may be forgetting to mention—and for this, mea culpa—I owe a very deep debt of gratitude for all of their assistance.

Thank you:

- To my daughters, Leah, Olivia, and Juliana, who know that they are the three most important people in the world to me. They have been so kind, loving, patient, and understanding, as I took so much time, too often away from them, to complete this book.
- To my mother, my late father, and my stepfather Stan Shepard, who—each in their own ways—have supported me since the day I was born and taught me how to be independent, to take risks, and to explore the world.
- To my brothers, Tom and Will, who have always been smarter people and better athletes than me, and who have believed so much in my work that they have sent several of their children with me to Africa, as I taught them to explore the world and to serve others in their formative years.
- To my best friend, Dan Kagan, who, as a friend and confidant, has helped me through thick and thin, something that is more than I can ever thank him for.
- To Sue, Joe ("Burch"), and Molly Burchard, whose belief in global IQ, and whose time together with me in the United

States and Africa has offered me the support I always needed through good times and bad.

- In memory of my cousin, Laura Olson Davidheiser, who was like a sister to me.
- To all of the teachers I have been so privileged to learn from as a student over the years; in Minneapolis while growing up, at Kenwood Elementary School, Jefferson Junior High School and West High School, especially Miss Brown (French), Mr. Oliver (French), Miss Westby (English), and Mr. Cherwin (my childhood piano teacher); at Middlebury College, especially Eric Davis, Mireille Barbaud-McWilliams, Carol Rifelj, and Nancy O'Connor; and at the Tufts Fletcher School, especially Leila Fawaz, Allen Henrikson, Bill Moomaw, and Jeswald Salacuse. I cannot thank these teachers and professors enough for sharing with me their passions, as I began to think about the idea of and importance of global IQ.
- To members of the Axis of Hope board of trustees and board of advisers for believing in this nonprofit organization and my vision for it.
- To dear friends at Belmont Hill School: Jian Gao, one of the best Chinese teachers in the United States, for her countless hours of interviews and class visits; Donna David, for her passion about service learning in other parts of the United States; former technology director John Thurner; Head of School Rick Melvoin; and school psychologist par excellence Michael Thompson.
- To other colleagues in the education world: Yu-lan Lin and Steven Berbeco of Boston Public Schools, Cheryl Johnson of the Woodstock School Chinese Program, Helena Curtain, and Ghislaine Boivigny of Lycée Louis-le-Grand in Paris.
- To so many of my former students and summer interns at Axis of Hope: especially Dan's son Max Kagan, Winston Esposito, Marcus Bullen, Joe "Burch" Burchard, Jake Mandelkorn, Ryan Miller, Frank Gorke, Joe Troderman, Steve Mahalec, Leslie Sale, and Stephanie Hagen.

- To my literary agent Joanne Wyckoff for remaining professional and keeping me laughing all along the way, from submitting the book proposal to Beacon Press to her patience when progress was at times slow.
- To Alexis Rizzuto, an incredibly bright, positive, patient, committed, and compassionate Beacon Press editor, for recognizing the merit in this book, for getting to know my passion for this material, for knowing how to listen to me and to understand me, and for her countless hours of reading and editing so well.
- To first cowriter Teresa Barker, for her talented writing assistance, and then to Stuart Horwitz. Stuart, an incredible writer, is sharp, kind, professional, and so much more. He understood just how to ask me the right questions, to get the valuable material that was needed, and to be patient when doing so. He has become a great friend as well—and we are already scheming about future collaborations!
- To Boston University colleagues Hardin Coleman, Tom Cottle, Scott Seider, and Amy Baltzell, and to MIT mentors Noam Chomsky and Suzanne Flynn, for their thoughtful ideas for the past four years.
- To members of the K–12 world who believed in me, in this book and in the organization Axis of Hope from the start: former NAIS president Pat Bassett, AoH Board Chair Joanne Hoffman, and teachers and administrators at Telluride Mountain School, Soundview School, Marin Country Day School, Out-of-Door Academy, and so many more schools across the United States.
- To my friend and primary care physician Jim Kolb, neurosurgeon and friend M. Peter Black, and the late Ed Bromfield, for believing in me and for helping me to stay in good health throughout this incredibly challenging, but successful journey.

Finally, thank you to all of the others who remain unnamed, but are still so greatly appreciated. You all, in your own special way, gave me the ability to complete this book.

Resources

Language Acquisition

Language Study

Middlebury Language Schools
Sunderland Language Center
Middlebury College
Middlebury, VT 05753
http://www.middlebury.edu/ls
languages@middlebury.edu
802-443-5510

Concordia Language Villages
901 8th St. S.
Moorhead, MN 56562
http://www.concordialanguagevillages.org/newsite
clv@cord.edu
800-222-4750

Language Teaching

American Council on the Teaching of Foreign Languages (ACTFL)
http://www.actfl.org
headquarters@actfl.org
703-894-2900

Travel and Service Learning

ACIS, including:

ENCORE Custom Performing Arts Tours and
AIFS Cultural Exchange (American Institute for Foreign Study)

http://www.acis.com
800-888-ACIS

AFS Intercultural Programs
http://www.afs.org
212-807-8686

EF Tours (Education First)
http://www.eftours.com
800-637-8222 (teachers)
877-205-9909 (students and parents)

Explorica
http://www.explorica.com
888-310-7120 (teachers)
888-310-7121 (travelers)

First Sports Tours
647 Beech Road
Auburn, NY 13021
315-253-0434

Global Explorers
http://www.globalexplorers.org
877-627-1425
877-627-1425

NETC (Educational Travel)
http://www.educationaltravel.com
800-771-2323

QUEST Adventures
PO Box 301233
Jamaica Plain, MA 02130
http://www.questadventures.org/
617-515-0492

Volunteers for Communities
http://www.sercap.org
866-928-3731

Case Studies (available from Axis of Hope)

"Whose Jerusalem? The Arab-Israeli Conflict"

"Rwanda: Reconciliation and Reconstruction, or Return to Conflict?"

"WE SAID AIDS! South Africa's Invisible Death"

"Burundi: A Genocide Ignored"

"China and Tibet: The Roof Is On Fire"

"The Democratic Republic of the Congo: Post-1994 Realities"

"Darfur: Division and Dissent in Western Sudan"

"Kashmir: Caught in the Cross-Fire"

"The Mexican Drug War"

"Mexico-US Immigration: Illegal or Not?"

"A Stumble Is Not a Fall: Post-Earthquake Haiti"

"An Offer She Could Not Refuse: Date Rape"

"The Kurds: A People Divided"

"The Colombia-US Cocaine War"

"Chechnya's Struggle for Independence"

Conflict Resolution

Axis of Hope
621 Commonwealth Avenue
Boston, MA, 02215
http://www.axisofhope.org
info@axisofhope.org
617-353-4794

Choices
The Choices Program
Brown University, Box 1948
Providence, RI 02912
http://www.choices.edu
choices@brown.edu
401-863-3155

Model UN
1800 Massachusetts Avenue NW, Suite 400
Washington, DC 20036
http://www.unausa.org/modelun
202-887-9040

Seeds of Peace
370 Lexington Avenue, Suite 2103
New York, NY 10017
http://www.seedsofpeace.org
info@seedsofpeace.org
212-573-8040

Workable Peace
238 Main Street, Suite 400
Cambridge, MA 02142
http://www.workablepeace.org
617-492-1414

Works Cited

Many of the direct quotes throughout the book are from the author's interviews.

Bedjaoui, Mohammed. "The Fundamentals of Preventive Diplomacy." In *Preventive Diplomacy: Stopping Wars Before They Start*. Kevin M. Cahill, ed. New York: Routledge, 2000.

Boutros-Ghali, Boutros. "An Agenda for Peace: Report of the Secretary-General." United Nations document A/47/277—S/24111. June 17, 1992, paragraph 21. www.un.org/.

Carter, Jimmy. *Talking Peace: A Vision for the Next Generation*. New York: Puffin, 1995.

Curtain, H. A., and C. A. Pesola. *Languages and Children—Making the Match*. Reading, MA: Addison-Wesley, 1988.

Dewey, John. *Democracy and Education*. New York: Free Press, 1997.

Dillon, Sam. "Foreign Languages Fade in Class—Except Chinese." *New York Times*, January 21, 2010.

Fisher, Roger, William L. Ury, and Bruce Patton. *Getting to YES: Negotiating Agreement Without Giving In*. New York: Penguin, 1991.

Freire, Paulo. *Pedagogy of the Oppressed*. New York: Continuum, 2000.

Fuchsen, M. "Starting Language Early: A Rationale." *FLESNews* 3, no. 1 (Spring 1989): 6–7.

George, Terry, director. *Hotel Rwanda*. MGM/United Artists, 2004.

Foreign Language Curriculum Task Force. *A Guide to Curriculum Planning in Foreign Language*. Madison: Wisconsin State Department of Public Instruction, 1986.

Guiora, Alexander Z., Robert C. L. Brannon, and Cecelia Y. Dull. "Empathy and Second Language Learning." *Language Learning* 22, no. 1 (June 1972): 111–30.

Hampton, Henry, producer. *Eyes on the Prize*. Blackside, Inc. 1987, 1990.

Heath, Chip, and Dan Heath. *Switch: How to Change Things When Change Is Hard*. New York: Crown, 2010.

Isenberg, Joan, and Nancy Quisenberry. "Play: A Necessity for All Children." *Childhood Education* 64, no. 3 (February 1988): 138–45.

Jeffers, Susan. *Feel the Fear and Do It Anyway*. New York: Ballantine, 1988.

Jones, Andrew. "Make or Break Time." *Guardian*, July 26, 2004.

Laurie, S. S. *Lectures on Language and Linguistic Method in the School.* University of Edinburgh, 1893.

Medalia, Hilla, director. *To Die in Jerusalem*. EJH Productions, HBO Documentary Films, New Israeli Foundation for Cinema and Television, Priddy Brothers, 2007.

Montessori, Maria. *The Absorbent Mind*. New York: Holt, 1995.

Peal, Elizabeth, and Wallace E. Lambert. *The Relation of Bilingualism to Intelligence*. Washington, DC: American Psychological Association, 1962.

Peck, Raoul, director. *Sometimes in April*. HBO Films, 2005.

Rich, Harvey L. *In the Moment: Embracing the Fullness of Life*. New York: William Morrow, 2002.

Spottiswoode, Roger, director. *Shake Hands with the Devil*. Head Gear Films, 2007.

Stone, Oliver. *Persona Non Grata*. HBO Series: America Undercover, 2003.

Suarez-Orozco, Marcelo M. "What Would Aristotle Think." Op-ed. *New York Times*, January 29, 2012.

Index